Paintbox Knits

MORE THAN **30** DESIGNS FOR KIDS

Paintbox Knits

MORE THAN 30 DESIGNS FOR KIDS

• • •

Mary H. Bonnette and Jo Lynne Murchland

Martingale
& COMPANY
WOODINVILLE, WASHINGTON

Credits

President . . . . Nancy J. Martin
CEO . . . . Daniel J. Martin
Publisher . . . . Jane Hamada
Editorial Director . . . . Mary V. Green
Editorial Project Manager . . . . Tina Cook
Design and Production Manager . . . Stan Green
Technical Editor . . . . Jane Townswick
Copy Editor . . . . Liz McGehee
Cover and Text Designer . . . . Trina Stahl
Illustrator . . . . Robin Strobel
Fashion Photographer . . . . Gloria Markel
Studio Photographer . . . . Brent Kane

Mission Statement

We are dedicated to
providing quality products and service
by working together to
inspire creativity and
to enrich the lives we touch.

Paintbox Knits: More Than 30 Designs for Kids

© 2001 by Mary H. Bonnette and Jo Lynne Murchland

Martingale & Company
20205 144th Avenue NE
Woodinville, WA 98072-8478 USA
www.martingale-pub.com

Printed in China
06 05 04 03 02 01   6 5 4 3 2 1

Library of Congress Cataloging-in-Publication Data
Bonnette, Mary H.
    Paintbox knits: more than 30 designs for kids / Mary
H. Bonnette and Jo Lynne Murchland.
       p. cm.
    ISBN 1-56477-336-1
       1. Knitting—Patterns. 2. Children's clothing.
    I. Murchland, Jo Lynne. II. Title.
TT825 .B65 2001
746.43'20432—dc21   00-050004

The straw hats shown on the cover were
purchased. No pattern is available.

Dedication

• • •

To Ashleigh and Savannah, who have been our ongoing inspiration
for designing bright and festive children's wear.
And just when they were getting too big to knit for, along came baby Rachel.

• • •

To our husbands, Harris and Gayle,
who were willing to take very long road trips,
driving all the way so that we could knit!
They have endured our K1, P2 conversations with humor,
patience, and a sense of pride.

Acknowledgments (in other words, thanks!)

• • •

Yarn Companies: Tahki; Stacey Charles, Inc.; Cascade Yarns; Dale of Norway; S R Kertzer; Trendsetter Yarns; and Blue Sky Alpacas

Button Companies: JHB International; Mill House Buttons by Gay Bowles; Trendsetter; and Sew Buttons, Inc.

Models: Savannah Bonnette, Ashleigh Cain, Rachel Cain, Callie Jones, Nicholas Jones, Max Molloy, Lely Molzan, and Lee Shen Molzan

Photography: Gloria Markel

• • •

We wish to thank each and every one of the kind and generous people who made contributions to this project. In many cases it was not convenient, but they gave us their very best. They understood that deadlines needed to be met and that photo shoots often had to be done in garments that did not correspond to the current season or temperature. Our models and photographer were real troupers, who worked through the heat, mosquitoes, and sand to give us the irresistible photos in this book. We are truly indebted to their parents. They arrived promptly and were prepared to act as hairdressers, prop managers, encouragers, entertainers, and feeders of the flock . . . raisins and Cheerios in every pocket. And to the yarn companies which saw that we had the yarns we needed in time to get our garments finished, we send a very grateful thank-you as well. We certainly could not have done it without you.

To Jane Townswick, our technical editor, we wish to express our sincere gratitude and appreciation. Her patience, expertise, and commitment to detail have amounted to an invaluable contribution to this book.

Contents

Introduction

As creative designers in the field of knitting, we decided in 1995 to start our own company, the Sassy Skein, and specialize in children's knitwear. It is worth noting that the concept for our company was driven by the dreams of two women with a combined knitting experience of more than sixty-five years. (Of course, we began knitting in the crib.) We devised our original business plan on a cocktail napkin in Key West, Florida. (A margarita or two may have been involved.)

We both had a strong vision of what we wanted to bring to the children's-knitwear market. Being career-oriented women, we coupled this vision with our love of knitting to take the Sassy Skein beyond the dreams expressed on that cocktail napkin. By concentrating on style and color, we began designing garments that were kid-friendly, with splashes and dashes of bright colors throughout. Let's face it—to design for a child, it helps to think like a child!

Designs by the Sassy Skein have an easily recognizable look, one that you may have spotted in many different knitting publications over the last several years. In addition, yarn shops throughout the country are now jazzing up their shelves with Sassy Skein patterns and kits that are known for their pizzazz, color, and great-fitting garments. We have also designed a collection of knitted garments for several premier yarn companies. Together, these companies and the Sassy Skein have created pattern booklets that maximize the potential of each company's yarns and color palettes. The same qualities that make our patterns so popular are featured in this book's designs.

Our goal is to bring you knitted garments that are uniquely suited to children's needs and that you will enjoy knitting. Because children are not merely miniature adults, we keep our focus on kid-friendly fibers, generous proportions, growing room, and wearability. This book provides you with patterns, techniques, and tips that will help you create colorful garments for the special little people in your life. For additional "how-to" knitting instructions, consult the books in our bibliography on page 142 or check out your local knitting shop for classes that will teach you the basics of knitting or help refine your already-acquired skills.

We sincerely hope that you have as much fun knitting these projects as we did designing them. We know your little ones will look great in their new hand knits!

Mary H. Bonnette and Jo Lynne Murchland

Knitting-Bag Essentials

Knitting a child's garment is fun and easy, especially when your knitting bag is stocked with tools that make each part of the knitting process successful. Following is a list of tools and supplies you'll want to have on hand for knitting the garments in this book.

Needles: We find that 24"-long circular needles (usually sizes 6, 8, and 10) are best for knitting the body of a toddler's or child's garment, while 16"-long circular needles work well for neck ribbings. You can often use straight needles, but we think that once you start using circular needles, you'll never want to put them down.

Tape measure: Any tape measure that is accurate will allow you to take the measurements you need to make a well-fitting child's garment.

Calculator: You should always do some periodic comparisons of your garment, making sure that it matches the pattern and your child's measurements. Since we do not all remember how to do long division in our heads, a calculator often comes in handy.

Stitch holders: You will need to place shoulder or neckline stitches on a stitch holder until you can knit the shoulder seams together or pick up stitches for the neck ribbing. You will need at least three stitch holders, each about 3" to 4" long, to make a sweater.

Stitch markers: Placing stitch markers in particular positions as you knit a child's garment makes it easy to keep track of stitches visually.

Needle end caps: Have you ever lost several inches of your next row from your needle? End caps will keep that from happening!

Gauge ruler: Measuring your own knitting gauge is an important part of knitting sweaters that fit well. Use a gauge ruler, so you can measure the number of your stitches and rows accurately.

Large-eyed sewing needles: These are great for sewing seams, pockets, and weaving in yarn ends.

Size F or G crochet hook: This medium-size crochet hook works well for adding single-crochet hems to children's garments.

Cable needle: For textured stitches, nothing is more indispensable than a cable needle that allows you to make cables easily.

Small scissors: Clipping yarn ends is quick and easy if you keep a small pair of scissors within easy reach, wherever you work.

Pencils or pens: Keep some sharpened pencils or pens handy for making notes about your pattern or keeping track of measurements.

Small notepad: Any kind of small notepad, with lines or without, will be helpful for jotting down notes while you work on a garment.

Graph paper: We like to use graph paper to help us visualize color changes and stitches for a complex pattern, make up our own graphed design, or catch a fleeting inspiration before it can get away.

Knitting for Fast-Growing Tykes

Here are a few tips to help you knit a sensational garment that will be as much fun to wear as it is to knit.

First, when choosing a pattern for a child, look for comfort features. Will it be nice and roomy? No child wants to be stuffed into a tight-fitting garment. Does the pattern you choose have a neck opening that will slip easily over the child's head? If the garment has cuffs or a waistband, are they going to be comfortable? If the child is a toddler, keep in mind that Mom may have to take the garment on and off several times during an outing. Can this be accomplished easily? Don't limit yourself to sweaters, either. There are any number of other knitted garments that look fabulous on children. Also take into consideration the difficulty of the pattern you choose. We all enjoy a knitting challenge, but for children, you will probably not be trying to create an heirloom for future generations.

Second, select a yarn that is comfortable to wear. Many children find beautiful wools scratchy and irritating. Also think about whether the garment will be worn over other clothing or directly against the child's skin. When knitting for a young child, think about using cotton yarn, which is comfortable, cool, and can be laundered easily. A young child will enjoy bright and bold colors more than intricate stitches. When it comes to kids, there are no color rules—be creative and have fun!

Third, look for designs that have a "built-in growth factor." Can cuffs be rolled back and unrolled later? Do shoulder straps on jumpers or rompers have button closures that can be let out as the child gets taller? Can the hem be let down?

Finally, take time to figure out how long it will take you to complete the garment. Decide what size you should make, based on the child's measurements and on the amount of time you will need to finish the garment. Consider how fast the child is growing (and they do grow fast!). Think about what season it will be when you finish knitting the garment. A beautiful size 2T wool sweater won't get much wear if you finish it in July.

Here is a handy checklist of things to think about whenever you want to make a knitted garment for a child.

Kids' Knits Dos and Don'ts

DO

- Read the care instructions on the yarn label.
- Wash your gauge swatches to check for shrinkage, stretching, and color bleeding.
- Adjust yarn requirements if you make changes to a pattern.
- Embellish knitted garments with buttons, ribbon, or doodads—kids love them! Be certain to sew them very securely.

DON'T

- Assume all cottons and wools are interchangeable; stitch gauges often vary, even in similar fibers.
- Assume knitwear is just for cold weather.
- Launder special buttons; remove them before washing the garment.

Time to Measure Up

BEFORE YOU begin any knitting project, measure the person for whom it is intended. Don't expect too much cooperation from little ones. Kids are generally far more interested in playing with the tape measure than standing still while you try to narrow their measurements down to the last quarter-inch. You can stand them up in front of their favorite cartoon, try bribery, threaten them with a bath, or catch them while they are sleeping—but somehow, you will need to come up with and write down accurate measurements for the following:

- Head circumference (necessary for more than just making a hat—you need to know if that sweater is going to fit over a child's head)
- Length from center back to top of one shoulder
- Length of arm from top of shoulder
- Wrist circumference
- Neck circumference (for a comfortable neckline)
- Chest
- Length from back of neck to waist
- For girls: length from back of neck to a comfortable hemline
- Waist
- Hips

This information will help you to decide which size to make your child's garment. It will also be a guide for making any adjustments for a tall, skinny child; a short, chubby tyke; or any other combination of features. Even if your garment is intended for a child who lives far away, get as much of this information as you can before starting a project. A surprise gift of a hand-knit sweater is wonderful; however, the "surprise" element may be yours if the finished garment doesn't fit well. Make every effort to obtain these measurements before you spend time and effort creating a beautiful knitted garment.

The finished sizes in the projects in this book are simply guidelines. Many factors influence how and why a garment is sized in a particular way. For example, an outer garment needs to be fuller and have more ease than an inner garment. In this book, you will find many dresses, jumpers, tunics, and rompers that are worn next to the skin and need a much finer degree of sizing. In addition, the lengths of different types of garments often vary according to the look that you are trying to achieve and the use of the garment. For example, a tunic may be longer than a sweater, even though they both fall into the sweater category. The styling features of a design also have a tremendous influence on its finished measurements. "Tally Ho!," shown on page 129, is an aviator-style jacket that is short and puffy, while "Teatime Teal," on page 103, is a jumper that emphasizes a sleek bodice and a shaped, full skirt. This attention in the design to the fit and style makes the garments in this book both distinctive and unique.

Making Adjustments for Fit

PAY CLOSE attention to the factors that help a garment fit, feel, and look better. A hands-on approach, involving measuring, trying on, customizing sleeve and garment lengths, or even changing colors, will make each project you knit completely yours. We design our garments with you and your child in mind, but only you can create a garment that expresses your own style.

As you work your way through the beginning stages of a project, take time to measure your garment 3" to 4" above the ribbing, so that you can be sure you are staying on target. If you have taken time to knit a gauge swatch (or swatches) and make sure that your knitting matches the stitch gauge indicated in the patterns, the fit of your garment is not likely to be a problem. Keep in mind that until the seaming and blocking are completed, you will only be working with approximate measurements.

Watch for the fit points in a garment, including the neck, head, cuff, and sleeve length. As you work, try the in-progress garment on your child from time to time. Keep in mind that before the ribbing is in place, the neck, cuff, and bottom garment openings are going to be larger than they will be in the finished garment. Take time to make sure that the neck opening will go over your child's head comfortably and that his or her hand will go through the cuff easily. If you notice a problem, you can adjust the number of stitches for the neck ribbing or cuff ribbing slightly. Obviously, if the fit is tight, you should add a few stitches, while if it is too loose, you can subtract a few stitches. To check sleeve length, measure the child from the center back of the neck to the top of the shoulder. Then take the measurement of the arm length and add these two measurements together. Now, lay your garment on a flat surface and measure it from the center back to the end of the sleeve. You can do this before or after you have worked the cuff. Adjust either the length of the sleeve or the length of the cuff, if necessary, to give a better fit. Even though you do not want the sleeves hanging to a child's knees, it is a good idea to build in some elbow room as well as some room to grow. One way to accomplish this is to make the cuff longer than necessary, so that it can be turned back or let down later with the next growth spurt.

Using Circular Needles

KNITTING WITH circular needles has a number of advantages when working on a project for a little body. Knitting in the round eliminates the need for side seams, which increases the garment's comfort level. Using circular needles is also faster than using straight needles, because circular needles are lightweight and not as cumbersome as straight needles. They are very flexible and easy to pack up and take with you anywhere you go.

Another advantage of knitting in the round is that the right side of your work is always facing you. This allows you to create a stockinette stitch by continuously knitting, rather than the traditional method of knitting one row, purling the next row, etc. Not only can the majority of your stitches always be knit stitches, but you can always see the right side of your work, which is helpful for keeping track of your pattern and visualizing a completed garment's size and shape.

Finally, you can use circular needles to knit back and forth without the awkwardness of having to turn your work at the end of every row. Give circular knitting a try! We think you will agree: it is fast, fun, and easy.

Picking Up Stitches

THIS TECHNIQUE has multiple applications in making the children's garments in this book. In most cases, it is the basis for neckline ribbing, button bands, and sleeves. The sleeves in this book are worked from the top down. This requires picking up stitches along the vertical edge of the front and back, and eliminates the need to sew sleeves into the garment. We feel that this is a much neater look and more comfortable for children's garments.

There are different schools of thought on the best technique for picking up stitches. After much trial and error, the following method is the one that we use and feel works best for the garments in this book. Unless instructed otherwise, always pick up stitches with the right side of the garment facing you. Using the right needle, insert the tip of the needle into the hole between the first and second stitch and pull up the loop. Using the color of yarn indicated, knit this stitch onto the right needle. Pull up the second stitch and continue in the same manner. Pick up and knit the required number of stitches as specified in your pattern.

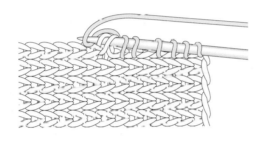

• • • • Tip • • • •

To be certain that the stitches you pick up are evenly spaced, divide the area you'll be working on into four equal sections and identify them with a marker. Then divide the total number of stitches to be picked up by four and let this number guide you as you pick up stitches throughout the four sections.

Knitting Shoulders Together

IF THERE is only one technique in this book that we suggest you try, this is it! Joining shoulder seams in this manner will give your garments the professional look of an expert knitter, and we think you'll use it for the rest of your knitting days.

Rather than binding off the shoulder stitches, place them on stitch holders. When you finish knitting the back and front of your garment, place them right sides together. Put the back shoulder stitches on one needle and the front shoulder stitches on a second needle, holding them in your left hand, with the needles pointed in the same direction. With a third needle in your right hand, insert the right needle into the first stitches on the needles in your left hand. Knit these two together at the same time. Repeat this step for the second stitches from each needle, giving you two stitches on the right needle. Then bind off the first stitch, bringing it over the second stitch on the right needle. Continue to knit two stitches together at a time from your left needles (one front stitch and one back stitch), and continue binding off after each successive stitch. When only one stitch remains on the right needle, break the yarn and pull it tightly through the final loop.

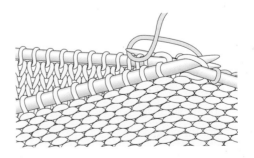

Weaving Side and Sleeve Seams

WE HAVE minimized the length of the seams for the garments in this book, to keep finishing challenges to a minimum. Sewing seams in the traditional manner leaves a thick seam, which can limit flexibility and ease of movement. Instead, we recommend the following method for weaving side and sleeve edges together.

Lay the garment edges together, right side up, on a flat surface. With a length of yarn, thread a large-eyed needle with a rounded tip. Begin by inserting the needle under the horizontal bar between the first and second stitches along the edge of one garment piece. Pull the yarn through. Cross over to the corresponding piece and insert the needle under the horizontal bar as for the first piece. Again, pull the length of yarn through firmly. Use just enough tension to draw the pieces together neatly, leaving flexibility in the seam. Continue in this manner, alternating from side to side, until the entire seam is woven together. In most cases, you can weave the sleeve and side seams together as one seam.

. . . . Tip . . .

Always work on a flat surface when weaving side and sleeve seams. Neatly finished seams are important to the look of the garment.

Making Buttonholes

FOR CHILDREN'S garments, buttonholes need to be sturdy. We like the K2tog, yo method of creating buttonholes, which you can reinforce with a single-crochet stitch if needed. Purchase your buttons before creating the buttonholes. Place buttonholes on the right side for a girl's garment, on the left side for a boy's garment. Keep in mind that many of the garments in this book are unisex, and while the buttonholes shown on the model garment may be on the wrong side for your child, it's easy to change this as you knit your garment. If you are undecided, make a pullover!

We also like the following method, especially for making buttonholes for larger buttons. The lower portion of the buttonhole is worked on the right side of the garment; the work is then turned, and the upper portion is worked from the wrong side of the garment.

1. Work as instructed in the project for buttonhole placement. Bring the working yarn to the front, slip the next stitch as if to purl, and return the yarn to the back of your work.

2. *Slip the next stitch from the left needle to the right needle, pass the first slipped stitch over the second slipped stitch, and drop it off the end of the needle. Repeat from * 1, 2, or 3 more

times, depending on the size of the buttonhole you need. Slip the last stitch on the right needle back to the left needle and turn your work.

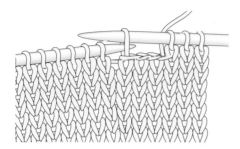

3. Using the following cable cast-on method, you will now be replacing the number of stitches that were just bound off, plus one stitch. Since you were given a choice of how large or small your buttonhole should be, it is important to know exactly how many stitches were bound off or eliminated in step 2. With the wrong side of your work facing you, move the yarn to the back of your work and proceed as follows: *Insert the right needle between the first and second stitches on the left needle, draw up a loop from the yarn that is held in the back of your work, and place it on the left needle. Repeat from * 1, 2, 3, or as many times as necessary to reinstate your original number of stitches, plus 1 additional stitch. Turn your work.

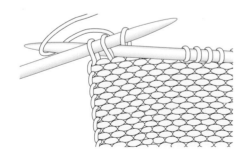

4. With the right side facing you and the working yarn in the back, slip the first stitch from the left needle and pass the extra cast-on stitch over it to close the buttonhole. You will now have the original stitch count and can proceed as instructed by the pattern.

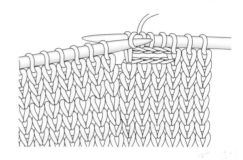

Spacing Buttonholes

SPACING BUTTONHOLES correctly is a simple math problem. For example, let's say your garment requires 5 buttons, and you will be working on 67 stitches. Since you have already purchased the buttons, you know that you need a 3-stitch buttonhole. Therefore, 15 (5 x 3 = 15) stitches of the button band will be used in buttonhole work. It is best to place the top and bottom buttons 2 or 3 stitches in from their respective edges. Let's do the math on a 67-stitch button band:

Leaving 2 sts each at top and bottom = 4 sts

Buttonholes with 3 sts each = 15 sts

Total sts needed to this point = 19 sts used, with 48 sts remaining

Placing the 3 remaining buttons on the button band will create 4 open segments on the band.

48 remaining sts ÷ 4 open segments = 12 sts each

The sequence for the evenly spaced buttonholes on this 67-st button band will be: 2 sts down from the top, *3 sts for the buttonhole, 12 sts for open segment; repeat from * 3 times, then add 3 sts for last buttonhole and 2 sts to bottom edge, for a total of 67 sts.

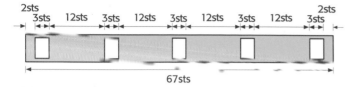

This technique also works for the K2tog, yo buttonhole method: use 2 sts for the buttonhole and proceed as described above. Before picking up stitches for a button band, work this math problem, using the number of stitches as instructed by the pattern. You may find, based on the number of stitches you use for each buttonhole, that you will need to adjust the number of stitches to be picked up by a stitch or two. Do not adjust this number by more than two stitches, or you will change the fit of the button band.

Single-Crochet Edges

A CROCHETED edge enhances a finished garment with a smooth, firm edge. It can also lend stability to a neckline, cuff, button band, collar, or—when worked in a contrasting color—become a decorative feature. If crochet work is among your many accomplishments, then you will have an opportunity to be versatile with your choice of stitches. However, a knitter need only know how to single crochet to achieve the benefits of a crocheted edge.

1. Working from right to left, insert the crochet hook into the first edge stitch, draw up a loop, wrap the yarn over the hook, and pull this loop through the first loop.

2. *Insert the hook into the next stitch, draw up a loop, wrap the yarn over the hook, and pull this loop through both loops; repeat from * until the bound-off edge has been covered.

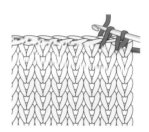

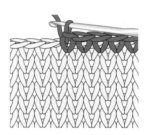

Tension is a significant factor in this procedure; you must adapt the size of the crocheted loops, as you pull them through, to the ease and stretch needed for the portion of the garment on which you are working. For example, necklines can be enhanced by a row of single crochet, but the resulting smooth, firm edge must have enough ease and stretch to allow a head to pass through comfortably. This might take a little practice. However, a crocheted edge has many applications for a knitter, and mastering this technique is well worth the effort.

Single-Crochet Chains

A SINGLE-CROCHET cord can be a useful addition to a garment. It can be woven through the waistband as a decorative drawstring to enhance its fit and stability, or it can be used as a decorative addition to buttonholes. Begin with a slipknot or loop, leaving a 6" tail of yarn. Insert a crochet hook through this first loop, from front to back. Wrap the working yarn over the hook and pull this new loop through, from back to front. Again, insert the crochet hook into the new loop from front to back, wrap yarn over the hook, and pull a new loop through, from back to front. Repeat this process until the specified length has been reached. On the last loop, break the yarn and insert through the open loop. Pull firmly.

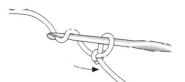

Wrap yarn over hook and
pull through loop.

Repeat, forming as many
chain stitches as desired.

Carrying Yarn on the Back of Your Work

MANY OF the garments in this book feature more than one color of yarn, which means that you will need to carry a different-color yarn across some stitches on the back side of your work. Follow these guidelines for weaving yarns together on the wrong side of a garment.

If you are working on the right side of the garment, drop the old color in the back, pick up the new color from under the old color, and work the stitches to the next color change. This will link the yarns together at the point where the yarn colors are changed.

When working on the wrong side of a garment, with the yarn in front of you, drop the old color, pick up the new color from under the old color, and work the stitches to the next color change.

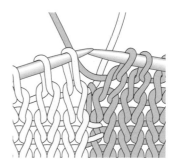

Right side of work

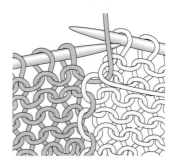

Wrong side of work

If you are working a design that has a long stretch of stitches in one color before you work with the other colors, you will need to carry or twist the unused colors every four to five stitches, without working them.

• • • • Tip • • • •

The key to success in using different colors is to carry the yarn very loosely across the back so that the natural stretch and flexibility of the knitted garment are not restricted. If the carried yarn is pulled too tightly, the garment will be too small. As you change colors and carry yarns, check your garment against the stitch gauge in the pattern to make sure you have allowed enough ease for a proper fit.

Another way to manage color knitting is to use bobbins for holding various yarns. This works especially well when a design is confined to small areas, such as pockets or collars—any area where there are long stretches of another color before the next design repeat occurs. Work the bobbin yarn into the pattern as needed, and leave it behind your work until you need to use it again on the next row.

For instructions, see pages 59–62.

Knitting from a Graph: Bottoms Up!

rEAD KNITTING GRAPHS from the bottom up unless otherwise instructed. Follow the graph from right to left on the right side of the garment, and from left to right on the wrong side of the garment. Each graph in this book features a key that explains what the symbols on the graph mean. There is also a color key.

Whenever you have a graphed motif to be placed evenly across a row (or round), take the number of stitches in the row and divide by the number of stitches for the graphed design. This will tell you how many stitches to place between each motif.

If you are instructed to place a motif vertically on a garment, determine the total number of rows for as many motifs as you want to include. Then use your own knitting gauge to determine the number of rows or inches you will need (vertically) in the section where the motifs are to be placed. Subtract the total number of motif rows from the total number of knitting rows. This will tell you how many rows you will have for spaces above, between, and below each motif.

Graphing Your Own Designs

HAVE YOU ever wanted to create your own sweater design? Has your little one ever asked, "Mommy, can you knit a bunny on my dress?" Or has Grandma ever thought about knitting coordinating boy and girl sweaters for Johnny and Julie, but didn't know how to go about the task?

Believe it or not, graphing a design and knitting from that graph is easier than you might think. Let's start with a "how-to" graph. Take your favorite small picture of a heart, bunny, truck, balloon, or whatever; a sheet of graph paper; and a sheet of carbon paper. You can buy graph paper and carbon paper at any office-supply store. There is even a knitter's graph paper on the market that matches stitch gauges. If you are considering graphing a complex design, we suggest using this type of graph paper, to ensure that the proportions are appropriate. But if your design is simple, standard graph paper will work fine.

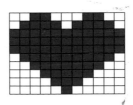

Knitter's graph paper

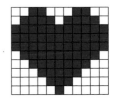

Regular graph paper

To get started, lay the graph paper on a solid surface. Place a carbon sheet (carbon side down) over it, and place the picture you want to trace (right side up) over both. Trace over the lines you want to copy on the graph paper. Using colored pencils, markers, or children's crayons, color in each block with the colors you want to use in your knitted garment. Each block represents a stitch. If you wish to use a variety of stitches, code your graph accordingly.

You can also design a graph by drawing directly on the graph paper, freehand. Start by drawing an outline of a design, and then color in the squares. This works well for repeat designs or geometric designs. Play with it and have fun!

If you don't want to tackle creating your own graph, look through cross-stitch and needlework books. You are sure to find some great graphs you can use in your knitting. Or choose designs you like from "Mix-and-Match Graphs," on pages 23–24.

Once you have created your graphed design, decide exactly where on the knitted garment you want to place the design. Check the pattern carefully for any stitch and/or row adjustments that will need to be made. Consider using your design as a single motif on the front of a sweater or on a pocket. Or repeat your design in the border of a skirt. Mix and match designs any way you wish. You are sure to end up with a one-of-a-kind knitted garment for that special little someone in your life!

For instructions, see pages 80–82 and 117–119.

Mix-and-Match Graphs

Small Flower
5 stitches x 5 rows

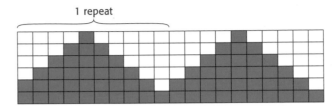

Triangle
10 stitches x 6 rows

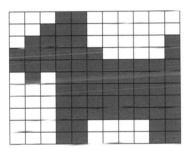

Scottie Dog
11 stitches x 11 rows

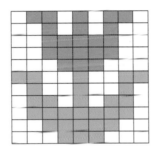

Large Flower
9 stitches x 11 rows

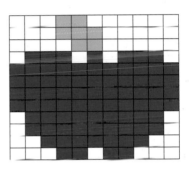

Apple
11 stitches x 12 rows

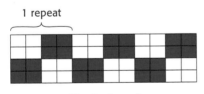

Checkerboard
4 stitches x 4 rows

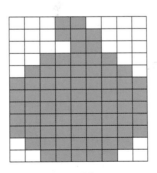

Pumpkin
9 stitches x 12 rows

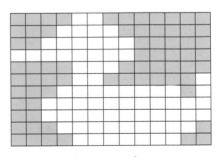

Large Duck
13 stitches x 11 rows

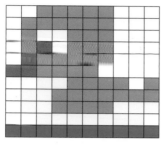

Small Duck
10 stitches x 11 rows

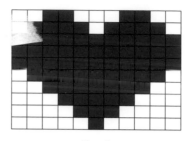

Heart
11 stitches x 10 rows

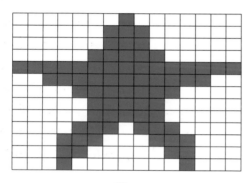

Star
15 stitches x 13 rows

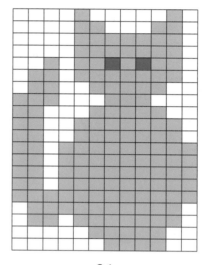

Cat
12 stitches x 20 rows

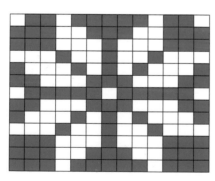

Snowflake
13 stitches x 13 rows

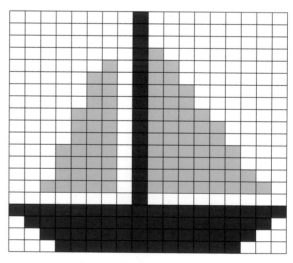

Sailboat
18 stitches x 20 rows

Y OU MAY THINK necklines are just necklines. A neckline doesn't really matter as long as the child's head will comfortably fit through. Not exactly so.

The shape and stitch of a neckline can dramatically change the appeal of a child's garment. Short necks may not look their best in high, flowing turtlenecks. Little, round faces may come alive with a gracefully curved sweetheart neckline. Boys like collars, and girls like ruffles, and everyone looks great in a V neck. So what is the secret to using necklines to individualize a garment for a child?

The mix-and-match potential of various standard necklines and stitches will give you many opportunities to be creative without taking a great deal of risk. The number of stitches given in the pattern can be worked as instructed, or in any number of creative ways. The following is just a sampling of possible pattern diversions from the standard ribbed crew neck.

borders or decorative stitching in the lower part of the garment, and by the time you get to the neck it's smooth sailing. To create a V neck, begin approximately 1½" to 2" before the instructions call for any neckline decreasing, find the middle of the front, attach another ball of yarn, and begin decreasing one stitch on each side of the middle, every other row. Check the number of stitches needed for the shoulder bind off and subtract that number from the number of stitches on the needle. When you have reached the number of stitches needed for the shoulder bind off, stop decreasing at the neck edge and continue to work until the garment measures the inches needed. When you pick up stitches for the neck edging, increase the number of stitches by approximately 25 percent.

Rolled Collar

THIS IS an easy variation on a crew neck. Pick up the number of stitches stated in the pattern; work K1, P1 ribbing or K2, P2 ribbing for 6 rows; now work in stockinette stitch for 8, 10, or 12 rows, depending on the yarn weight. Bind off in a contrasting color for pizzazz. The neckline will roll over and show the wrong side of the stockinette stitch.

V Neck

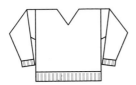

A V NECK is not for every garment, especially if there is a stitch or color pattern that should not be interrupted. However, many kids' patterns feature

Split Collar

THIS NECKLINE IS great for boys or girls and ever so easy. Pick up the number of stitches stated in the pattern, beginning at the center front. Work back and forth in your preferred stitch until the collar measures approximately 3½" to 4½". According to the decor of the garment, this collar can be done in stripes, one color, or edged in an accent color.

Turtleneck

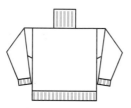

CONSIDER THE use of the garment and the weight of the yarn in choosing this neckline variation. While turtlenecks are great for adults, children have very short necks and may not like them as much. However, there is definitely a time and place for a turtleneck in a child's wardrobe. If your yarn is very bulky, keep the length a little shorter than usual. If the stitch gauge is not less than 5 to 5½ stitches per inch, the garment is a good candidate for a turtleneck. Measure your child to see how many inches it will take for a nice, high neck

that will turn over to a length that falls below the line where the neck stitches were picked up. Bind off loosely, remembering that the full length of this tube must be expandable enough for your child's head to slide through easily. The best stitch for this neckline is the K1, P1 rib or the K2, P2 rib. Other stitches may compromise the turtleneck look.

Ruffled Neck

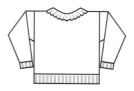

SOMETIMES THIS neckline really sets a garment off—maybe because it's a little different. Pick up the number of stitches per the pattern instructions. In Row 1, increase 2 stitches in every stitch on the needle. A ruffled neckline needs to be short. Depending on the number of rows you knit to the inch, work approximately 1" to 1½" and bind off. This neckline works best in a rib stitch: K2, P2 or K3, P3.

Varying a neckline can individualize a garment, and so can varying the stitch. The stitch needs to be flexible but stable so that the neckline holds its shape and stays flat. A few choices to consider include garter stitch; seed stitch; K1, P1; K2, P2 baby-cable ribbing or mock-cable ribbing; braided ribbing; twisted ribbing; and fisherman's ribbing. These stitches can be done without any modifications to the original pattern instructions, except for adding or subtracting a stitch to accommodate the odd- or even-number specifications of the chosen ribbing.

Creative Embellishments

fOLLOWING ARE A few of the ways we like to use buttons and tassels for creating interesting looks in kids' knitted garments.

Buttons

BUTTONS COME in all shapes and sizes, which makes them great for dressing up a child's garment. There are some unique, kid-friendly buttons on the market. Using brightly colored or unusual buttons can transform a cute hand-knitted sweater into a true work of art. Consider the following ideas when working on your next project.

- Use the same button but in different colors or sizes to add interest.

- Pick a theme, such as farm animals, then choose a variety of different, coordinating buttons for the garment.

- Double up a large and a small button; sew one on top of the other.

- Consider adding an interesting button to the bodice of a sweater as a decorative touch. To change the look, use a shank button and pin it from the wrong side of the sweater. That way you can switch the button to create a different look. (You can also remove the button for laundering.)

- When sewing on four-hole buttons, use a contrasting colored yarn and crisscross the yarn through the holes.

Tassels

TASSELS ARE fun to make and are great decorative elements for kids' knits. All you need to do is wrap a strand of yarn uniformly around an index card or piece of cardboard that is as long as you want your finished tassel to be. Wrap the yarn around the card many times for a full look in the finished tassel. Insert a separate piece of yarn through the wound yarn, and tie it tightly in the middle. Slide the wound yarn off the index card or piece of cardboard, and cut to the length desired. Trim the tassel until the yarn ends are even, and attach to the garment with a crochet hook.

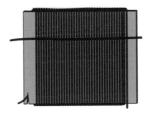 

Blocking Kids' Knits

THE PROFESSIONAL LOOK that comes from blocking a knitted garment is well worth the time and effort it takes. The yarn label is the first place to look for information that will help you choose the best method for blocking your finished garment. Since children's knitwear is rarely made with "dry clean only" yarns, the blocking process usually involves steaming or spraying the garment with water.

To block by spraying water on a garment, use a clean spray bottle and mist the garment with water. This will straighten the seams, cables, and pockets, and will shape the shoulders and neckline. Pin the garment to a flat surface, such as an ironing board or a towel on a bed, taking care to avoid stretching or distorting the stitches.

To block a garment with steam, heat an iron or steamer to a temperature that conforms to the information on the yarn label. Turn the garment wrong side out and place it on a flat surface. Holding the iron or steamer close to the garment, steam it thoroughly. Pin the garment to a flat surface and allow it to dry thoroughly.

. . . . . Tip . . .

Do not steam cables, ribbing, textured, or raised stitches, as steaming tends to alter their shape.

On some occasions, wetting and shaping a garment can produce the best blocking results. Following instructions on the yarn label, thoroughly wet the garment in a tub of water and then remove and roll it in a large towel to remove the excess water. Being careful not to stretch the garment, place it on a flat surface and shape and pin it as for the spray or steam methods. Keep the garment out of direct sunlight and direct heat, and allow it to dry completely.

For instructions, see pages 126–128.

Caring for Children's Sweaters

ET'S FACE IT: kids will be kids, and their garments are likely to end up on the laundry-room floor. When you purchase yarn for a project, keep in mind the properties of that yarn and check the label on the skeins to find out whether it can withstand machine washing. Avoid expensive "dry clean only" yarns and go for cottons, washable wools, blends, or acrylics. These yarns can all be machine washed, and in some cases even tumbled dry on a cool setting.

If you plan to machine wash a knitted garment (gentle cycle only), do not put it in with a regular load of clothes, because different weights of clothing may stretch and distort it. It can be helpful to put a towel in the washer when you wash a knitted garment, to protect it from wrapping around the agitator.

In many cases, it is probably just easier to hand wash kids' knits, so you can control stress on the garment and tell immediately if spots, stains, and dirt are coming out. Unless you are dealing with an all-white garment, do not use chlorine bleach under any circumstances. Cool to cold water is preferable for all garments, especially those with many colors.

A small amount of fabric softener may be used to help keep the garment soft and to put a little fluff in the fiber. Dry flat on a towel or on a mesh garment dryer, out of bright light and away from an artificial heat source.

When it is time to store a garment away for future use, wash the garment and place it in a protective bag or storage box. Ventilated vegetable bags are perfect for this use. Fold the garment carefully, place acid-free tissue paper between the layers, and slip it into a bag or box. It is best to have a well-ventilated and temperature-controlled space for this kind of storage. Don't relegate the garment to a damp basement or a frigid (or sweltering) attic.

Your hand knits are a labor of love for a very special person in your life. Care for them properly and they will be around for many years of continued enjoyment.

For instructions, see pages 129–132.

What to Do with Leftover Yarns

WE ARE ALL guilty of the irresistible urge to save leftovers, whether it is food, old shoes, monogrammed towels, or yarn. Many books have been written on how to rid your life of clutter, and yet, no matter what, we knitters hold onto our stash of yarns. Maybe it is because we yearn for the day when there will be nothing else to do but prop up our feet, turn on some music, pour a glass of lemonade—and knit. Okay, so we all admit that we can't be cured. It's time to find a quick, useful—and if need be, portable—project for the next vacation, the next doctor's appointment, the next football game, the next five minutes.

There are many small projects that don't require matched dye lots, or in some cases, even matched stitch gauges. Children's knitwear can be the perfect place to do your spring housecleaning. There are so many kids' knits that require just a touch of color here or a touch of texture there. The skimmer is a child's sweater that can be 7", 8", or 9" long; it is meant to be short, so that a fat little tummy shows. Make it sleeveless if you are running out of yarn, or change colors and make the sleeves each a different color. Remember, kids love color! If your climate is such that a tummy will get chilly if it is hanging out, make hats—striped, color-blocked, with bulky brims or pompons. Soft, cuddly animals are another good project for leftover yarns; the textures and colors in your stash will probably make great whiskers, tails, noses, furry feet, antlers, and tongues. A whole knitted zoo could be lurking in your storage chest, just waiting to get loose. And then there are always doll clothes—even for G.I. Joe! From a cape for Superman to a bikini for Barbie doll, there are lots of dolls just waiting for clothing that shows your special touch. We hope that this book will give your imagination a nudge and inspire you to have fun as you create a wide array of wonderful kids' knits.

For instructions, see pages 35–37.

The Patterns

. . .

Dominoes

This black-and-white domino design, with accents of
coral and green, is a winner for both boys and girls.
You may substitute the colors of your choice or knit
the sweater in all black-and-white.

Dominoes

This pattern is sized 2T (3T, 4T, 6).

●

FINISHED MEASUREMENTS

Chest: 24 (26, 28, 30)"

Length: 12½ (14½, 16½, 18)"

Drop Sleeve: 9½ (10½, 11½, 12½)"

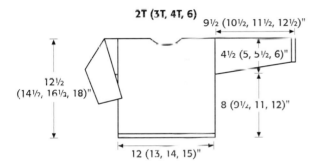

2T (3T, 4T, 6)

9½ (10½, 11½, 12½)"

4½ (5, 5½, 6)"

12½ (14½, 16½, 18)"

8 (9¼, 11, 12)"

12 (13, 14, 15)"

Materials

- Tahki Cotton Classic, 50-gram skeins (108 yds), 100% cotton
  Color A   3 (3, 4, 4) skeins #3002 Black
  Color B   2 (3, 3, 3) skeins #3001 White
  Color C   1 (1, 1, 1) skein #3475 Coral
  Color D   1 (1, 1, 1) skein #3726 Green
- Size 6 needles: circular (24" and 16"). If desired, straight needles can also be used.
- Stitch holders
- Stitch markers

Gauge

22 stitches and 28 rows = 4" in pattern stitch

To save time, always check your gauge. If necessary, change needle size to obtain correct gauge.

Pattern Stitch

Seed Stitch (even number of stitches)

Row 1 (RS): K1, P1 across row.

Row 2 (WS): Purl the knit sts and knit the purl sts.

Repeat Rows 1 and 2.

Front

THIS SWEATER is not knitted in the round, but you can use circular needles if you wish. Wind Colors A, B, and C from skeins into 2 separate balls each, for a total of 6 balls of yarn.

Rows 1–4 (6): In Color A, CO 66 (72, 78, 84) sts. Work in seed st for 4 (4, 6, 6) rows. Row 5 (7): In Color C, purl across row.

Row 6 (8) (RS): Beg color pattern as follows: In Color B, seed st on 3sts; in Color B, K16 (17, 18, 20) sts; in Color C, P1 (1, 2, 2) sts; in Color A, K4 (5, 6, 6) sts; in Color B, K4 (5, 6, 6) sts; in Color C, P1 (1, 2, 2) sts; in Color A, K34 (37, 38, 42) sts; in Color A, seed st on 3 sts.

Row 7 (9) (WS): Staying in color patt as est for last row, seed st on first and last 3 sts and purl all sts in between.

Continue working a repeat of last 2 rows for 14 (14, 18, 20) rows.

Next row: Work through Color C sts; reverse black and white colors for "domino" sts (see photo, page 32); and cont across row in patt as est. When garment measures 3½", discontinue seed st on the 3 sts on each side; work these sts as St sts. Cont working in patt, reversing "domino" color sts every 14 (14, 18, 20) rows until garment measures 10½ (12½, 14, 15 ½)".

Front Neck Shaping

WORK ACROSS 21 (23, 25, 26) sts; place 24 (26, 28, 32) sts on st holder for neck opening; attach Color A and work across rem 21 (23, 25, 26) sts. Working on left shoulder sts, dec 1 st at neck edge every other row 2x. Cont on rem sts until garment measures 12½ (14½, 16½, 18)". BO shoulder sts or place on st holder for seam method of preference.

Back

Rows 1–5 (7): In Color A, CO 66 (72, 78, 84) sts and work 4 (4, 6, 6) rows in seed st and 1 purl row in Color C, as for front.

Row 6 (8): In Color A, seed st on 3 sts; K30 (33, 36, 39) sts; in Color B, K30 (33, 36, 39) sts; Seed st on 3 sts.

Work garment in St st with 3 sts on each end in seed st for 3½". Discontinue seed st; cont in St st on all sts until garment measures 12 (14, 16, 17½)", ending with WS row.

Back Neck Shaping

WORK 20 (22, 24, 25) sts; place 26 (28, 30, 34) sts on st holder; attach Color B yarn and work 20 (22, 24, 25) sts for second shoulder. Cont on each shoulder, dec 1 st at neck edge 1x. When garment measures 12½ (14½, 16½, 18)", BO shoulder sts or place on st holder for seam method of preference. Join shoulder seams.

Sleeves

THE SLEEVES are knitted from the top down. They are not knitted in the round, but you can use circular needles if you wish. Measure 4½ (5, 5½, 6)" in both directions from shoulder seam and insert a st marker. Matching sleeve color to sweater body and with RS facing you, PU 48 (52, 56, 62) sts evenly between markers.

Color A Sleeve: Work in St st until sleeve measures 5 (6, 6, 7)". On next row, beg dec 1 st at each edge every sixth row 2 (2, 3, 3)x. Cont in St st until sleeve measures 9 (10, 11, 12)". On next row, dec 8 (8, 8, 10) sts evenly across row. On rem 36 (40, 42, 46) sts, seed st for 5 rows. BO loosely.

Color B Sleeve: Work in St st until sleeve measures 5 (6, 6, 7)". Cont in St st until sleeve measures 7 (8, 9, 10)", ending with WS row. Next row, in Color D, seed st on 2 rows. On next row, beg alternating 4 sts in Color A and 4 sts in Color B to end of row. Cont this checkerboard patt with Color A and Color B for 4 rows. In Color D, knit 1 row and work next row in K1, P1 across. In Color B, work 4 rows in St st, dec 8 (8, 8, 10) sts evenly across last row. On rem sts, seed st for 5 rows. BO loosely.

Neck Edge

THE NECK is worked in the round. Use 16" circular needles. Beg at Color A shoulder seam, in Color A, PU 80 (84, 88, 92) sts around neck edge, including sts on back and front st holders. K2, P2 for 3 (3, 5, 5) rounds. Work in St st for 6 (6, 8, 8) rounds. BO loosely.

Finishing

SEW SLEEVE and side seams above seed st tog, leaving side vents open. To create numbers on "dominoes," add French knots in contrasting colors: thread needle with appropriate yarn color and bring point of needle up from wrong side of garment where you wish to place a French knot. Do not bring needle completely through; wrap yarn around needle 2x. Bring needle up just enough so that you can turn it and reinsert it very close to the spot where it came up. Bring yarn completely through to wrong side of garment, creating a French knot on right side of garment. Leave tails of yarn on WS until all French knots are completed. Tie off and cut yarn tails to approx ½". Do not weave yarn tails into garment.

A stylish twist on an old classic, this Argyle sweater is perfect for a crisp cotton yarn. Use bobbins to complete the color work.

Argyle

This pattern is sized 2T (4T, 6)

●

FINISHED MEASUREMENTS

Chest: 22 (26, 32)"

Length: 12 (15, 17)"

Drop Sleeve: 10 (11, 12)"

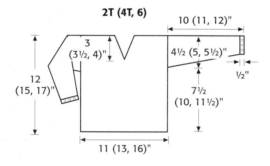

2T (4T, 6)

Materials

- Dale of Norway Kolibri, 50-gram skeins (113 yds), 100 percent Egyptian cotton
  Color A   5 (5, 6) skeins #0020 Ecru
  Color B   1 (1, 1) skein #3209 Orange
  Color C   1 (1, 1) skein #2208 Yellow
  Color D   1 (1, 1) skein #7936 Green
- Size 5 needles: circular (24" and 16") or straight
- Bobbins
- Stitch holders
- Stitch markers

Gauge

24 stitches and 30 rows = 4" in rib st
To save time, always check your gauge. If necessary, change needle size to obtain correct gauge.

Pattern Stitch

Seed Stitch

Row 1 (RS): K1, P1 across row.

Row 2 (WS): Purl the knit sts and knit the purl sts.

Repeat Rows 1 and 2.

Back

THIS SWEATER is not knitted in the round, but you can use circular needles if you wish. In Color A, CO 66 (78, 96) sts.

Rows 1–3: Work in seed st.

Row 4: K3, P3; repeat across row.

Row 5: Purl all sts.

Repeat Rows 4–5 until garment measures 5 (7½, 9)", ending with RS row.

Next row: Purl and inc 0 (2, 0) sts and dec 2 (0, 0) sts to adjust st count for Argyle Sweater Design. Wind Colors B, C, and D onto several bobbins, making sure to wind enough bobbins in each color, so you can carry the yarn across short distances on the WS.

Referring to Graph #1, repeat 32-st design until 4 (5, 6) lower diamonds and 4 (5, 6) upper diamonds (29 rows) are in place. Colors can be alternated or repeated. At the completion of the Argyle Sweater Design, in Color A, repeat K3, P3, as for bottom, inc 2 (0, 0) sts and dec 0 (2, 0) sts in first row. Cont in patt until garment measures 11½ (14½, 16½)".

Next row: Work patt across 21 (25, 33) shoulder sts; work next 24 (28, 30) sts and place on st holder for neck; work rem 21 (25, 33) sts. Cont patt on each shoulder, dec 1 st at neck edge every row 2x. When garment measures 12 (15, 17)", BO shoulder sts or place on st holder for seam method of preference.

Front

WORK AS for back to completion of Argyle Sweater Design, ending with RS row.

Next row (WS): In Color A, repeat K3, P3 patt, inc 2 (0, 0) sts and dec 0 (2, 0) sts in row.

V-Neck Shaping

NEXT ROW (RS): Divide sts into 2 equal sections of 33 (39, 48) sts each. Attach second ball of yarn and work each section in patt, dec 1 st at neck edge EOR 14 (16, 17)x. Cont even on each side until garment measures 12 (15, 17)". BO shoulder sts or place on st holder for seam method of preference. Join shoulder seams.

Sleeves

THE SLEEVES are knitted from the top down. They are not knitted in the round, but you can use circular needles if you wish. Measure 4½ (5, 5½)" from shoulder seam in both directions, and insert a st marker. With RS facing, in Color A, PU 54 (60, 66) sts evenly between st markers. Work in K3, P3 ribbing until sleeve measures 3 (4, 4)". Beg dec 1 st at each edge every fourth row 6 (6, 9)x. When sleeve measures 6½ (7½, 8½)", follow Graph #2 at right for 14-row Argyle Sleeve Design. Cont in rib patt until sleeve measures 9½ (10½, 11½)". On next row, dec 6 (8, 8) sts evenly across row. Work 3 rows of seed st. BO.

Neck Edge

BEG AT CENTER front, PU 92 (98, 106) sts around neck edge with 16" circular needles, including sts on back holder. Work 3 rows in seed st. BO in seed st.

Finishing

SEW SLEEVE and side seams tog. At neck front, lap edges over each another and stitch down to secure.

Graph #1: Argyle Sweater Design

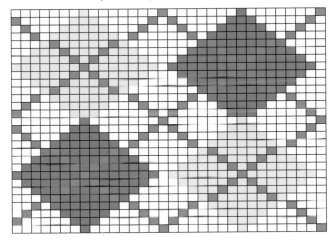

Argyle Sweater Design is 32 stitches x 29 rows; repeat to make 4 (5, 6) diamonds across sweater front and back. Work design in St st.

Graph #2: Argyle Sleeve Design

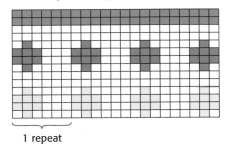

1 repeat

Argyle Sleeve Design is worked on the knit stitches of the rib and repeated as needed for sleeves.

Color Key

Color A: Ecru   Color C: Orange

Color B: Yellow   Color D: Green

Flowermania

Bright Tahki Cotton Classic yarn in oranges, reds, and yellows inspired this little sweater. Always a conversation piece!

Flowermania

This pattern is sized 18M (2T, 3T, 4T).

●

FINISHED MEASUREMENTS

Chest: 24 (26, 27, 28)"

Length: 11 (12, 13, 14)"

Drop Sleeve: 9 (10, 11, 12)"

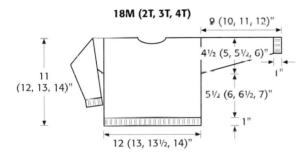

18M (2T, 3T, 4T)

Materials

- Tahki Cotton Classic, 50-gram skeins (108 yds), 100% cotton

Color A	2 (2, 3, 3) skeins	#3553 Dk. Yellow
Color B	1 (1, 1, 2) skeins	#3402 Orange
Color C	1 (1, 1, 1) skein	#3997 Red
Color D	1 (1, 1, 1) skein	#3533 Light Yellow
Color E	1 (1, 1, 1) skein	#3472 Green

- Size 6 needles: circular (24" and 16")
- Stitch holders
- Stitch markers

Gauge

22 stitches and 28 rows = 4" in pattern stitch

To save time, always check your gauge. If necessary, change needle size to obtain correct gauge.

Pattern Stitches

SEE THE 2 design graphs on page 40.

Back and Front

THIS GARMENT is knitted in the round on circular needles.

Rounds 1–8: In Color A, CO 132 (142, 148, 154) sts. Work in K1, P1 ribbing for 8 rounds.

Rounds 9–11: St st in Color B.

Round 12: St st in Color A.

Rounds 13–14: St st in Color C.

On next round, work Small Flower Design (Graph #1). After flowers are in place, work 2 rounds in Color C; 1 round in Color A; 3 (4, 5, 6) rounds in Color B; 1 round in Color A; 5 (6, 7, 8) rounds in Color C; 1 round in Color A; 3 (4, 5, 6) rounds in Color B; 1 round in Color A. At this point, divide sts into 2 sections for front and back (placing extra st, if needed, in back). Place back sts on st holder. Cont on front sts, working back and forth, as on a straight needle.

Front

STAYING IN St st, work 2 rows in Color C. Work Large Flower Design (Graph #2). After flowers are in place, work 2 rows in Color C; 1 row in Color A; 3 (4, 5, 6) rows in Color B. Beg neck shaping.

Front Neck Shaping

On NEXT row, in Color A, work 22 (23, 24, 24) sts, place next 22 (25, 26, 29) sts on st holder. Attach second ball of yarn and work rem 22 (23, 24, 24) sts. Working shoulders at same time, cont in St st, dec 1 st every row at each neck edge 4x and staying in the following stripe pattern: 3 (4, 5, 6) rows in Color B; 1 row in Color A; 2 rows in Color C; 1 row in Color A. BO shoulder sts or place on st holder for seam method of preference.

Back

PU BACK sts from holder and follow stripe pattern as in front, omitting front neck shaping. When back measures the same as finished front, beg back shoulder and neck shaping.

Back Shoulder and Neck Shaping

WITH RS facing you, BO the 18 (19, 20, 20) shoulder sts for each shoulder and sew shoulder seams tog, or place them on a st holder and knit the shoulder sts tog. Place rem center sts on a st holder. The shaping comes from working the shoulders together, or sewing them, which gives them a slight drop from the neck edge. (For a child this slight bit of shaping is all you need.)

Sleeves

THE SLEEVES are knitted from the top down. Measure 4½ (5, 5½, 6)" in both directions from shoulder seam, and insert a st marker.

Right Sleeve: With RS facing, in Color A, PU 50 (55, 60, 66) sts evenly spaced between st markers. Work in Color A in St st until sleeve measures 8 (9, 10, 11)". On next row, dec 9 (12, 13, 15) sts evenly across. On rem sts, work in K1, P1 ribbing for 7 rows. BO for cuff.

Left Sleeve: In Color A, work in St st until sleeve measures 5 (6, 7, 8)". Work 2 rows of St st in Color C. Work Small Flower Design (Graph #1), placing 5 (5, 6, 6) flowers evenly around sleeve. After flowers are completed, work 2 rows of St st in Color C. Cont St st in Color A until sleeve measures 8 (9, 10, 11)". On next row, dec 9 (12, 13, 15) sts evenly across. Work in K1, P1 ribbing for 7 rows. BO for cuff.

Neck Ribbing

WITH RS of garment facing you, in Color A, PU 80 (86, 90, 96) sts for neck edging. Work in K1, P1 ribbing for 4 rows. BO edging in K1, P1.

Finishing

SEW SIDE and sleeve seams tog.

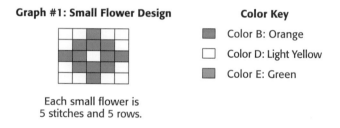

Graph #1: Small Flower Design

Color Key
- Color B: Orange
- Color D: Light Yellow
- Color E: Green

Each small flower is
5 stitches and 5 rows.

Place 7 (7, 7, 8) small flowers around front and back.

Graph #2: Large Flower Design

Each large flower is
7 stitches and 15 rows.

Place 7 (7, 7, 8) large flowers around front and back.

You'll love knitting this one—it goes really fast! We liked this Tahki cotton yarn and decided to try using two strands together, one in yellow and one in orange, for an interesting color effect. Double stranding meant that this sweater could be worked on larger needles.

Sun-Kissed

This pattern is sized 2T (4T, 6).

●

FINISHED MEASUREMENTS
Chest: 26 (28, 30)"
Length: 11 (13, 15)"
Sleeve: 10 (13, 14)"

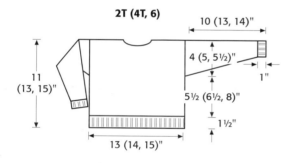

2T (4T, 6)

11 (13, 15)"

10 (13, 14)"

4 (5, 5½)"

1"

5½ (6½, 8)"

1½"

13 (14, 15)"

Materials

- Tahki Cotton Classic, 50-gram skeins (108 yds), 100% cotton
Color A 2401	3 (4, 4) skeins Orange
Color B 2553	3 (4, 4) skeins Yellow
Color C 2997	1 (1, 1) skein Red
- Size 10 needles: circular (24")
- Size 6 needles: circular (16"). If desired, straight needles can be used for the sleeves.
- 2 stitch holders
- Large-eyed sewing needle
- 2 yellow buttons (buttons shown are JHB)

Gauge

16 stitches and 20 rows = 4" in pattern stitch

To save time, always check your gauge. If necessary, change needle size to obtain correct gauge.

Front and Back

THIS SWEATER is knitted in the round, using 2 strands of yarn and circular needles. With 2 strands of Color A and size 10 circular needles, CO 104 (112, 120) sts.

Rounds 1–6: K1, P1 ribbing around.

Round 7: Switch to 1 strand of Color A and 1 strand of Color B; K1, P1 around.

Round 8: Knit around.

Repeat Rounds 7and 8 until sweater measures 7 (8, 9½)". Divide sts into 2 equal sections for front and back. Place back sts on a st holder. You will now be working back and forth on the needle (you can still use your circular needles). Working with front sts, cont in patt st until front measures 9 (11, 13)", ending on WS row. Beg front neck shaping.

Front Neck Shaping

WITH RS facing, work across first 18 (19, 20) sts for shoulder, place center 16 (18, 20) sts on holder. Join second ball of yarn and work across second shoulder. Cont working in patt st, dec 1 st at each neck edge every row 4x. Work shoulder sections until front measures 11 (13, 15)". BO shoulders.

Back

PU STS from holder and work in same st patt as front, omitting neck shaping until back measures 11 (13, 15)". BO shoulders. Join shoulder seams.

Collar Edging

WITH RS of garment facing, in a single strand of Color A and using 16" size 6 circular needles, PU 54 (58, 62) sts around neck opening, including those sts on holders, for neck edging. Working in the round, knit 6 rounds. BO loosely. Let collar roll out.

Sleeves

THE SLEEVES are knitted from the top down. They are not knitted in the round, but you can use circular needles if you wish.

Right sleeve: With RS facing, in the same 2 colors as for sweater body, PU 40 (44, 48) sts evenly around opening. Work in patt st until sleeve measures 10 (12, 13)", dec 6 (8, 10) sts evenly across last row. Work 6 rows of K1, P1 ribbing for cuff. BO in ribbing.

Left sleeve: Work as for right sleeve for 5 (6, 6½)". Add 3 stripes as follows: Staying in patt, work 2 rows using 2 strands of Color B, and 2 rows using 2 strands of Color A. Repeat these 4 rows 2x more. Then, return to same 2 colors as for upper portion of sleeve, and work in patt until sleeve measures 10 (12, 13)", dec 6 (8, 10) sts evenly across last row. Work 6 rows of K1, P1 ribbing for cuff. BO in ribbing.

Pocket

WITH 2 strands of Color C and size 10 circular needles, starting 1" from edge of ribbing in lower left corner of sweater front, PU 14 sts. Work in St st for 2". Work 4 final rows of K1, P1 ribbing. BO. Sew sides of pocket down. Sew a button on each upper corner of pocket.

Finishing

SEW SLEEVE seams together. Block sweater carefully.

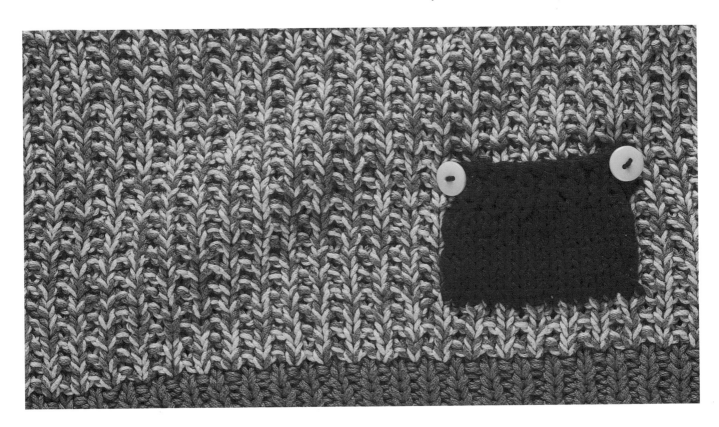

Lazy Daisy

Here's a wonderfully simple variation on the traditional
cardigan, inspired by these great flower buttons.
The simple tie closure makes this one easy—no buttonholes to fuss with.

Lazy Daisy

This pattern is sized 18M (2T, 3T, 4T).

●

FINISHED MEASUREMENTS

Chest: 24 (26, 27, 28)"

Length: 11 (12, 13, 14)"

Sleeve: 9 (10, 11, 12)"

18M (2T, 3T, 4T)

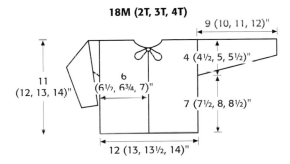

Materials

- Cascade Yarn's Madil Cotton Cable, 50-gram skeins (123 yds), 100% cotton
  Color A #566   5 (5, 6, 7) skeins Yellow
  Color B #001   Small amount of White
  Color C #563   Small amount of Green

- Size 5 needles: circular (24" and 16") or straight. If desired, straight needles can be used for the sleeves.

- Stitch holders

- Size G crochet hook

- Large-eyed sewing needle

- 3 daisy buttons (buttons shown are Trendsetter)

Gauge

22 stitches and 28 rows = 4" in pattern stitches

To save time, always check your gauge. If necessary, change needle size to obtain correct gauge.

Pattern Stitches

Moss Stitch

Row 1 (RS): K2, P2 across.

Row 2 (WS): Purl the knit sts and knit the purl sts.

Row 3 (RS): P2, K2 across.

Row 4 (WS): Knit the purl sts and purl the knit sts.

Repeat this 4-row pattern.

Seed Stitch

Row 1 (RS): K1, P1 across row.

Row 2 (WS): Purl the knit sts and knit the purl sts.

Repeat Rows 1 and 2.

Front and Back

THIS SWEATER is not knitted in the round, but you can use circular needles if you wish. On size 5 needles in Color A, CO 132 (144, 148, 154) sts. Work in moss st until sweater measures 7 (7½, 8, 8½)". Divide sts into 3 sections, creating back section and 2 front sections. Back section is 68 (72, 76, 78) sts; each front section is 32 (36, 36, 38) sts. With yarn attached to each section, cont working each section in patt st until front sections measure 9½ (10½, 11½, 12½)". Place back section on st holder. Beg front neck shaping.

Front Neck Shaping

AT EACH front neck edge, BO 8 (9, 10, 11) sts. Cont to work in patt, dec 1 st every row at each neck edge 6x. Work rem 18 (21, 21, 22) sts, until each front measures 11 (12, 13, 14)". BO shoulder sts or place on st holder for seam method of preference.

Back Neck Shaping

PICKING UP sts from st holder, cont working in patt until back measures 11 (12, 13, 14)". BO all of the back sts. Sew shoulder seams tog.

Sleeves

THE SLEEVES are knitted from the top down. They are not knitted in the round, but you can use circular needles if you wish. In Color A, with RS facing, PU 46 (50, 54, 60) sts, dividing sts evenly around armhole. Work in patt st until sleeve measures 6 (7, 8, 9)". On next row beg dec 1 st at each edge every third row 5 (6, 6, 6)x. BO cuff.

Front Tie

RIGHT FRONT tie: In Color A, with RS facing, PU 7 sts along right front edge near neckline. Work in K1, P1 seed st until tie measures 4". Dec 1 st on each edge until you have used all the sts.

Left front tie: Repeat along left front.

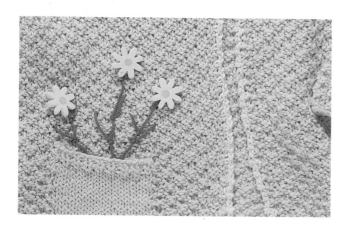

Pocket

ON RIGHT front, with RS facing, PU 22 sts 1" from sweater bottom. Work pocket in St st until it is 2" long. Work final 4 rows in K2, P2 ribbing. BO in K2, P2. Sew sides of pocket to sweater front.

Finishing

SEW SIDE and sleeve seams tog. In Color B, single crochet around sweater hem, up the front, around neck, and back down other front. Using 3 daisy buttons, in Color C, create a design of flowers coming out of the pocket, embroidering the stems in stem stitch.

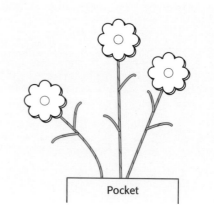

Pocket

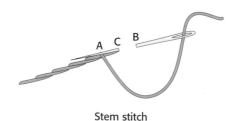

Stem stitch

This ladybug is a lucky find for any girl or boy! We
chose an acrylic yarn to keep this white sweater easy
to launder.

Little Ladybug

This pattern is sized 18M (2T, 4T, 6).

•

FINISHED MEASUREMENTS

Chest: 24 (26, 28, 30)"

Length: 13 (14, 15, 16)"

Sleeve: 9 (10, 12, 14)"

18M (2T, 4T, 6)

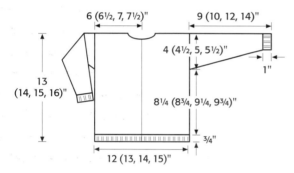

6 (6½, 7, 7½)" 9 (10, 12, 14)"

4 (4½, 5, 5½)"

1"

13 (14, 15, 16)"

8¼ (8¾, 9¼, 9¾)"

¾"

12 (13, 14, 15)"

Materials

- Ornaghi Elle, 50-gram skeins (145 yds), 100% acrylic yarn

Color A #44	1 (1, 1, 1) skein Black
Color B #29	1 (1, 1, 1) skein Red
Color C #20	3 (3, 4, 5) skeins White

- Size 5 needles: circular (24" and 16") or straight
- Stitch holders
- Cable needle
- 5 (5, 6, 6) black-and-white checked buttons (buttons shown are Sew Buttons)

Gauge

22 stitches and 28 rows = 4" in St st

To save time, always check your gauge. If necessary, change needle size to obtain correct gauge.

Pattern Stitches

4-Stitch Cable

Row 1: K4, *K1, P1, K1, K4 (for cable); repeat from *.

Row 2: P4, *P1, K1, P1, P4 (for cable), repeat from *.

Repeat these 2 rows 3x for a total of 8 rows.

Row 9: K4, *K1, P1, K1, put 2 K sts on a cable needle and hold in front of work; K2 sts; K2 sts from cable needle, repeat from * across.

Seed Stitch

Row 1 (RS): K1, P1 across row.

Row 2 (WS): Purl the knit sts and knit the purl sts.

Repeat Rows 1 and 2.

Front and Back

THIS SWEATER is a "mock cardigan." It is not knitted in the round, but you can use circular needles if you wish. In Color B, CO 134 (144, 154, 164) sts.

Rows 1–4: Work in K2, P2 ribbing.

Rows 5–6: In Color C, work in St st.

Row 7: In Color A, K2, P2 across.

Row 8: In Color B, purl across.

Row 9: Using Colors A and C, alternate K2 sts in each color across.

Row 10: Repeat Row 8.

Beg sweater body cable pattern as follows:

Row 1: K4, *K1, P1, K1, K4 (for cable), repeat from * across until 10 sts rem; knit rem sts.

Row 2: P4, *P1, K1, P1, P4 (for cable), repeat from * across until 10 sts rem; purl rem sts.

Repeat these 2 rows, crossing the cables every 9th row as follows: K4, *K1, P1, K1, put 2 K sts on a cable needle and hold in front of work; K2 sts; K2 sts from cable needle, repeat from * across, until 10 sts rem; knit rem sts.

Cont in 4-st cable patt, and on the next row begin knitting the Ladybug pattern on the last 10 sts. Knit a total of 4 (5, 5, 6) ladybugs up the left front edge of the sweater, referring to the Ladybug graph below right. When garment measures 9 (9½, 10, 10½)", divide into 3 sections as follows: 68 (72, 78, 82) sts for back and 33 (36, 38, 41) sts for each front. Place back sts on st holder. Working on both front sections at the same time, cont in patt until fronts measure 10½ (11½, 12½, 13½)". Beg front neck shaping.

Front Neck Shaping

BO FIRST 8 (10, 12, 14) sts at each neck edge. Cont working in patt, dec 1 st at each neck edge every row 6x. When front measures 13 (14, 15, 16)", BO shoulder sts or place on st holder for seam method of preference.

Back

PU BACK sts from st holder. Work in patt until back measures 13 (14, 15, 16)". BO 19 (20, 20, 21) sts for each shoulder or place sts on a st holder for seam method of preference. Place center sts on st holder. Join shoulder seams.

Button Band

WITH RS facing, in Color B, PU 60 (66, 70, 76) sts along left front. Work in K1, P1 seed st for 5 rows. BO in K1, P1 ribbing. Do not knit a right button band. To create the "mock cardigan" look, lay button band slightly over the right front and use Color B to sew button band in place.

Neck Edging

WITH RS of garment facing, in Color C, PU 80 (90, 100, 105) sts, including those on st holders for neck edging. Work in the round for 3 rounds in K1, P1 ribbing. BO.

Sleeves

SLEEVES ARE knitted from the top down. They are not knitted in the round, but you can use circular needles if you wish. With RS facing, in Color C, PU 44 (50, 55, 60) sts. Work in St st. When sleeve measures 6½ (7½, 9½, 11½)", work next row in Color B and work 1 row in Color C. Switching to Color A, K1, P1 across. Still working in Color A, dec 10 (12, 14, 16) sts evenly across row. In Color B, work 5 final rows of K2, P2 ribbing for cuff. BO.

Finishing

SEW SLEEVE and side seams tog. Position 5 (5, 6, 6) buttons evenly down button band and tack down with Color B.

Ladybug Graph

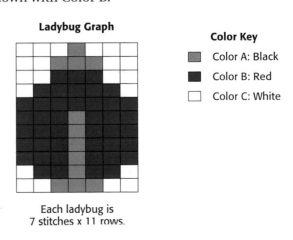

Color Key

Color A: Black
Color B: Red
Color C: White

Each ladybug is
7 stitches x 11 rows.

Woolly Worm

This sweater is good bait for a compliment. We combined a multicolored, textured yarn with a solid-colored cotton to create real eye appeal in a garment that's great for both girls and boys.

Woolly Worm

This pattern is sized 18M (2T, 4T, 6).

•

FINISHED MEASUREMENTS

Chest: 24 (26, 28, 30)"

Length: 11 (13, 15, 17)"

Sleeve: 9 (10, 11, 13)"

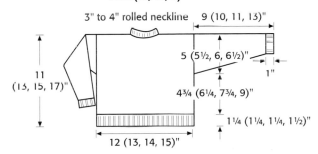

18M (2T, 4T, 6)

3" to 4" rolled neckline   9 (10, 11, 13)"

5 (5½, 6, 6½)"

1"

11 (13, 15, 17)"

4¾ (6¼, 7¾, 9)"

1¼ (1¼, 1¼, 1½)"

12 (13, 14, 15)"

Materials

- Tahki Cotton Classic, 50-gram skeins (108 yds), 100% cotton
  Color A   2 (3, 3, 4) skeins #3997 Red
- S R Kertzer's Magic Garden Buttons, 50-gram skeins (153 yds), 83% wool/17% polyester
  Color B   1 (2, 2, 2) skeins #876 Blue
  Color C   1 (1, 1, 1) skein #877 Yellow
- Size 6 and 7 needles: circular (24" and 16"). If desired, straight needles can be used for the sleeves.

- 2 buttons (optional; buttons shown are JHB International)
- Stitch holders
- Stitch markers

Gauge

21 stitches and 36 rows = 4" for sweater body

22½ stitches and 40 rows = 4" in garter st for sleeves

To save time, always check your gauge. If necessary, change needle size to obtain correct gauge.

Back

THIS SWEATER is not knitted in the round, but you can use circular needles if you wish. On size 6 needles, in Color B, CO 62 (68, 74, 80) sts.

Work in K1, P1 ribbing as follows:

Color B, 2 rows; Color C, 1 row; Color A, 6 (6, 6, 8) rows.

On size 7 needle, work 4 rows as follows:

Row 1: *In Color C, K1; in Color A, K1; repeat from * across row.

Row 2: *In Color B, P1; in Color C, P1; repeat from * across row.

Row 3: In Color A, knit across.

Row 4: Purl across.

Beg garment pattern on multiple of 6 sts plus 2:

Row 1 (RS): In Color B, K1, *K6, sl 2 wyib, K2, sl 2 wyib; repeat from *, end K1.

Row 2 (size 18M and 4T): In Color B, K1, *sl 2 wyif, K2, sl 2 wyif, K6; repeat from *; end K1.

Row 2 (size 2T and 6): In Color B, K1, *K6, sl 2 wyif, K2, sl 2 wyif; repeat from *; end K1.

Row 3: In Color A, knit across.

Row 4: In Color A, purl across.

Row 5: In Color B, K1, *sl 2 wyib, K2, sl 2 wyib, K6; repeat from *; end K1.

Row 6 (size 18 mo. and 4T): In Color B, K1 *K6, sl 2 wyif, K2, sl 2 wyif; repeat from *; end K1.

Row 6 (size 2T and 6): In Color B, K1, *sl 2 wyif, K2, sl 2 wyif, K6; repeat from *; end K1.

Rows 7–10: In Color A, St st 4 rows.

Rows 11–20: Repeat Rows 1–10, but work Color B rows in Color C. Color A rows rem in Color A.

Cont in this 20-row repeat until garment measures 10½ (12½, 14½, 16½)".

Next row: Work patt on 17 (18, 21, 23) sts; place 28 (32, 32, 34) sts on st holder; attach yarn to work rem sts. Dec 1 st at each neck edge 1x and cont on shoulder sts until garment measures 11 (13, 15, 17)". BO shoulder sts or place on st holder for seam method of preference.

Front

WORK FRONT same as back until front measures 9½ (11½, 13, 15)".

Next row: Work across 20 (21, 24, 26) sts; place 22 (26, 26, 28) sts on st holder; attach second ball of yarn and cont across row. Work in est patt, dec 1 st each side of neck EOR 4x. Cont on shoulder sts until garment measures 11 (13, 15, 17)". BO shoulder sts or place on st holder for seam method of preference. Join shoulder seams.

Sleeves

THE SLEEVES are knitted from the top down. They are not knitted in the round, but you can use size 7 circular needles if you wish. For the sleeves, use S R Kertzer's Magic Garden Buttons. Measure 5 (5½, 6, 6½)" in both directions from shoulder seam and insert a st marker. With RS facing, in Color B, pick up 50 (56, 62, 68) sts evenly between front st markers. In Color B, work in garter st (knit every row) until sleeve measures 3 (3, 3½, 4½)". Next row, beg dec 1 st at each edge every sixth row 4 (5, 5, 6)x. Cont in garter st until sleeve measures 5½ (6½, 7½, 9½)". In Color A, cont in patt 2 rows; in Color C, cont in patt 14 rows. Dec 6 (8, 10, 12) sts evenly in last row of Color C. Cuff is worked on size 6 needle in K1, P1 ribbing for 9 rows in Color A; 1 row in Color C, and 2 rows in Color B. BO loosely.

Rolled Neck Ribbing

USING SIZE 6 circular needles and Color C, with RS of garment facing, PU 78 (82, 86, 92) sts, including sts on back and front st holders. Ribbing is worked in the round as follows: K1, P1 for 4 rounds; on size 7 needles, St st for 8 rounds; in Color B, St st for 1 round. BO loosely in Color B.

Mock Neck Rib (optional)

IN COLOR C, CO 20 sts and K1, P1 for 5 rows, using size 6 needles. BO. Stitch down to center front of garment and add 2 decorative buttons to give the appearance of a neck opening.

Finishing

SEW SIDE and sleeve seams tog.

Biker Babe/Biker Boy

Rev up those needles, and hit the road knitting! Not into Harley? Substitute two other colors and you have a great striped sweater.

Biker Babe/Biker Boy

This pattern is sized 2T (4T, 6, 8).

●

FINISHED MEASUREMENTS

Chest: 27 (29, 31, 33)"

Length: 13 (14, 16, 17)"

Drop Sleeve: 10 (11, 13, 14)"

2T (4T, 6, 8)

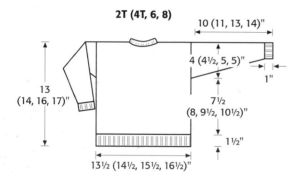

Materials

- Tahki Cotton Classic, 50-gram skeins (108 yds), 100% cotton

  Biker Babe Color Pattern
  Color A   2 (2, 3, 3) skeins #3002 Black
  Color B   3 (4, 5, 6) skeins #3202 Orange

  Biker Boy Color Pattern
  Color A   3 (4, 5, 6) skeins #3002 Black
  Color B   2 (2, 3, 3) skeins #3202 Orange

- Size 6 needles: circular (24" and 16"). If desired, straight needles can be used for the sleeves.

- Stitch holders
- Harley-Davidson appliqué patch (optional; purchase at your local Harley-Davidson store)
- Sewing needle and thread

Gauge

22 stitches and 28 rows = 4" in pattern stitch
To save time, always check your gauge. If necessary, change needle size to obtain correct gauge.

Front and Back

BOTH VERSIONS of this sweater are knitted in the round. For either version, in Color A, CO 150 (160, 170, 180) sts. Work in K2, P2 ribbing for 10 (10, 12, 12) rows. Beg color stripe patt as follows:

Biker Babe

Round 1: In Color B, knit around.

Round 2: K1, P1 around.

Rounds 3–8: Knit around.

Round 9: P1, K1 around.

Round 10: Knit around.

Rounds 11–13: In Color A, knit around.

Repeat these 13 rounds.

Biker Boy

Round 1: In Color B, knit around.

Round 2: In Color A, *K1, sl 1 Color B st, repeat from * around.

Rounds 3–5: In Color A, knit around.

Round 6: In Color B, knit around.

Round 7: Repeat Round 2.

Rounds 8–10: Alternating Colors A and B, knit around to create a checkerboard patt.

Rounds 11–16: In Color A, knit around.

Repeat these 16 rounds.

Cont working in stripe patt until garment measures 9 (9½, 11, 12)". At this point, divide sts into 2 sections for front and back. Place back sts on st holder. Working back and forth on the needles with front sts, cont in stripe patt until front measures 11 (12, 14, 15)". Beg front neck shaping.

Front Neck Shaping

WITH RS facing, work across the 25 (27, 28, 30) left shoulder sts in patt. Place center 25 (26, 29, 30) sts on a st holder. Join second ball of yarn and work across other shoulder in patt. Cont to work in patt, dec 1 st at each neck edge every row 5x until front measures 13 (14, 16, 17)". BO shoulder sts or place on st holder for seam method of preference.

Back

WITH RS facing, PU sts from holder and work in stripe patt until back measures 13 (14, 16, 17)". BO the 20 (22, 23, 25) shoulder sts or place them on a st holder for seam method of preference. Place center 35 (36, 39, 40) sts on holder. Join shoulder seams.

Rolled Neck Edging

WITH RS of garment facing, in Color B for Biker Babe or in Color A for Biker Boy, PU 78 (82, 86, 90) sts around neck, including those on st holders. Working in the round, K 7 (8, 8, 9) rounds. BO loosely.

Sleeves

THE SLEEVES are knitted from the top down. They are not knitted in the round, but you can use circular needles if you wish. With RS facing, in Color B for Biker Babe and in Color A for Biker Boy,

PU 45 (50, 55, 55) sts evenly around armhole. For Biker Babe, work in same stripe patt as sweater body. For Biker Boy, work St st in Color A until you reach final 3 rows (based on the measurements of the child you are knitting for). Inserting the other color, alternate colors for the checkerboard patt used in sweater body. You will be working back and forth on the needles. Cont until sleeve measures 9 (10, 12, 13)". On the next knit row, dec 10 (11, 12, 12) sts evenly across row. In Color A, work 6 rows of K2, P2 ribbing for cuff. BO in K2, P2.

Finishing

SEW SLEEVE seams tog. Block lightly. Sew Harley-Davidson patch on sweater front if desired.

Autumn Harvest

Whether a child is picking apples or raking leaves, this warm and fuzzy turtleneck is a season stealer. The leaf design was stamped with a rubber stamp onto a piece of graph paper. (Easy!) The patch on the front can be changed or removed for yet another look.

Autumn Harvest

This pattern is sized 18M (2T, 4T, 6).

•

FINISHED MEASUREMENTS

Chest: 24 (26, 28, 30)"

Length: 13 (14, 15, 16)"

Sleeve: 9 (10, 12, 14)"

18M (2T, 4T, 6)

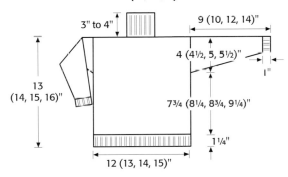

Materials

- Blue Sky Alpaca, 100% alpaca yarn, 120 yds, 2 oz. or 60 grams

Color A	2 (2, 3, 3) skeins Gold
Color B	1 (1, 2, 2) skeins Brown
Color C	1 (1, 1, 1) skein Green
Color D	2 (2, 2, 2) skeins Spice
Color E	1 (1, 1, 1) skein Red
Color F	1 (1, 1, 1) skein Ecru
	(optional for patch)

- Size 6 needles: circular (24" and 16"). If desired, straight needles can be used for the sleeves.

- Stitch holders
- Large-eyed needle

Gauge

22 stitches and 28 rows = 4" in pattern stitch
To save time, always check your gauge. If necessary, change needle size to obtain correct gauge.

Pattern Stitches

Moss Stitch

Row 1 (RS): K1, P1 across.

Row 2 (WS): Purl the knit sts and knit the purl sts.

Row 3 (RS): P1, K1 across.

Row 4 (WS): Knit the purl sts and purl the knit sts.

Repeat this 4-row pattern.

Garter Stitch

Knit every row.

Front and Back

THIS GARMENT is knitted in the round. In Color A, CO 134 (144, 154, 164) sts.

Rounds 1–3: K2, P2 around.

Round 4: Cont in rib patt, work every other 2 sts in Color C.

Rounds 5–9: In Color A, work in K2, P2 ribbing.

Beg sweater body. Front is worked in Color A in moss st. Back is worked in Color B in garter st. Cont until garment measures 9 (9½, 10, 10½)". Divide into 2 sections to create armholes. Place back sts on st holder. Working in patt on front sts (you will now be working back and forth on the needle), cont until sweater front measures 10 (11, 12, 13)". Switch to Color C, and beg working K2, P2 ribbing for shoulder. When front measures 10½ (11½, 12½, 13½)", beg front neck shaping.

Front Neck Shaping

WITH RS facing, work across 23 (25, 25, 27) sts for first shoulder, placing center 21 (22, 27, 28) sts on a st holder; cont across second shoulder. Cont working in Color C, dec 1 st at each neck edge every row 5 (5, 6, 6)x. When front measures 13 (14, 15, 16)", BO the 23 (25, 25, 27) shoulder sts or place them on a st holder for seam method of preference. Join shoulder seams.

Back

PU BACK sts from st holder. In Color B, work in garter st until back measures 10 (11, 12, 13)". Switch to Color C and work in K2, P2 ribbing as for front shoulder until back measures 13 (14, 15, 16)". BO the 23 (25, 25, 27) shoulder sts or place them on a st holder for seam method of preference. Place center 31 (34, 39, 40) sts on holder. Join shoulder seams.

Turtleneck Edging

WITH RS of garment facing you, in Color E, PU 76 (80, 86, 90) sts, including those on st holders for neck edging. Work in the round in K1, P1 ribbing for 3" to 4". BO loosely. Fold collar over.

Sleeves

THE SLEEVES are knitted from the top down. They are not knitted in the round, but you can use circular needles if you wish. In Color D, PU 44 (50, 55, 60) sts. Work in St st until sleeve measures 8 (9, 11, 13)". On next K row, dec 8 (10, 12, 14) sts evenly across row. Work final rows of K2, P2 ribbing for cuff. BO in K2, P2 ribbing.

Leaf Patch

FOLLOW LEAF graph to knit leaf patch. Block completed leaf patch carefully and overstitch it onto sweater front, using Color B. With Color C, overstitch leaf stem and veins.

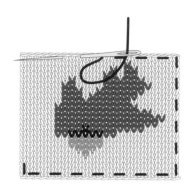

Finishing

SEW SLEEVE seams tog. Block sweater carefully.

Leaf Graph

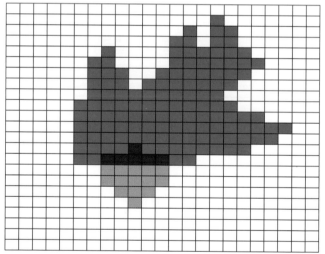

Leaf patch is 23 stitches x 23 rows.

Color Key

- ■ Color B: Brown
- ■ Color D: Spice
- □ Color F: Ecru
- ■ Color G: Taupe

Triangle Treat Pullover

Bold geometric shapes are perfect for children's garments. These chunky triangles are so easy to knit, you may want to use them again and again.

Triangle Treat Pullover

This pattern is sized 2T (3T, 4T).

●

FINISHED MEASUREMENTS

Chest: 26 (27, 28)"

Length: 12 (13, 14)"

Sleeve: 10 (11, 12)"

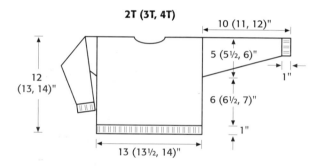

2T (3T, 4T)

10 (11, 12)"

5 (5½, 6)"

1"

12 (13, 14)"

6 (6½, 7)"

1"

13 (13½, 14)"

Materials

- Tahki Cotton Classic, 50-gram skeins (108 yds), 100% cotton (or any yarn that will meet the stitch gauge)
  Color A   3 (4,5) skeins #3874 Blue
  Color B   1 (1,1) skein #3726 Lime Green
  Color C   1 (1, 1) skein #3533 Yellow
- Size 6 needles: circular (24" and 16") or straight
- 4 buttons (buttons shown are JHB)
- Stitch holders
- Stitch markers
- Bobbins (optional)

Gauge

22 stitches and 28 rows = 4" in pattern stitch
To save time, always check your gauge. If necessary, change needle size to obtain correct gauge.

Front Pattern

SEE GRAPHS for triangle and circle design placements. Wind yarn for graphed designs on bobbins if desired.

Front

THIS SWEATER is not knitted in the round, but you can use circular needles if you wish. In Color A, CO 72 (76, 80) sts.

> Row 1: P2, K2 across row.
>
> Row 2: Work all sts as presented.
>
> Rows 3–7: Repeat Rows 1 and 2.
>
> Row 8 (RS): Knit across row, inc 1 st.
>
> Row 9: Purl across row.
>
> Row 10: In color A, K12 (14, 16) sts; in Color C, insert Large Triangle Design (see Graph #1); in Color A, knit rem 12 (14, 16) sts. Stay in St st and Large Triangle patt as est in Graph #1 until front measures 7 (8, 9)". Work designs from Graph #2 and Graph #3 as directed on graphs and, at the same time, cont on Graph #1 if necessary. When front measures 10 (10½, 11½)", ending WS, beg front neck and shoulder shaping.

Front Neck and Shoulder Shaping

NEXT ROW: Work 23 (24, 25) sts for left shoulder; place 27 (29, 31) center sts on st holder; place 23 (24, 25) sts for right shoulder on second st holder.

Left shoulder: Working shoulder sts, cont with Graph #2 as est, dec 1 st at neck edge EOR 2x. Work rem 21 (22, 23) sts until left front measures 11½ (12½, 13½)". In next row, place 3 buttonholes (K2tog, yo), evenly spaced, across shoulder, referring to pages 16–18. Cont in St st for 3 rows. BO shoulder sts loosely. Right shoulder: PU sts from second st holder, attach yarn at inside edge, and work across row; cont with Graph #3 as est. Dec as for left shoulder, omit buttonholes, and cont in St st until garment measures 12 (13, 14)". BO loosely.

Back

In Color A, CO 72 (76, 80) sts. Repeat Rows 1–7, working back ribbing same as front. In Color A, work in St st until back measures 12 (13, 14)", ending WS row. Next row, BO 21 (22, 23) sts for right shoulder; place 30 (32, 34) center sts on holder; purl rem 21 (22, 23) sts for left shoulder. Work 6 rows in St st for shoulder flap extension. BO loosely. Join right shoulder seams. Join left shoulder from outside edge to first buttonhole.

Sleeves

The sleeves are knitted from the top down. They are not knitted in the round, but you can use circular needles if you wish. Measure 5 (5½, 6)" from shoulder seam in both directions and insert a st marker. With RS facing, in Color A, pick up 54 (60, 66) sts evenly between markers. Purl return WS row. Stripes are each 7 rows. Right sleeve is worked in alternating stripes of Color A and Color C. Left sleeve is worked in alternating stripes of Color A and Color B. Cont until sleeve measures 5 (6, 7)". On next row, beg dec 1 st at each edge every fourth row 5 (6, 7)x. When sleeve measures 9 (10, 11)", dec 6 (6, 8) sts in row. On rem 38 (42, 44) sts, beg ribbing. Using alternate color from last stripe (stripe does not have to be complete), work K2, P2 ribbing for 7 rows. BO loosely.

Neck Edge

In Color A and using 16" needle, with RS of garment facing, beg at left shoulder edge and PU 82 (86, 94) sts, including sts on holder, around neck edge. Work in K2, P2 ribbing for 3 rows. In patt, place buttonhole (K2, yo) in ribbing at left shoulder edge in line with previously worked buttonholes. For more information on buttonholes, see page 16. Cont in rib patt until a total of 7 rows have been completed. BO neck sts loosely.

Finishing

Sew side and sleeve seams tog. Sew buttons on back left shoulder flap to correspond with buttonholes. Block carefully.

Graph #2: Circle

Circle design is 16 stitches x 28 rows.
Place in garment when front measures 7 (8, 9)".
On right side row, knit 24 (25, 26) stitches;
begin Graph #2; continue across row as est.

Graph #1: Large Triangle

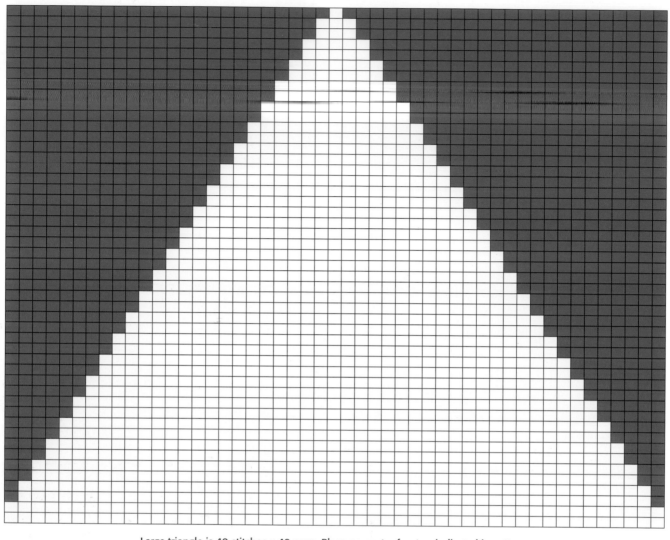

Large triangle is 49 stitches x 49 rows. Place on center front as indicated in pattern.

Color Key

- ■ Color A: Blue
- ▨ Color B: Lime Green
- □ Color C: Yellow

Graph #3: Small Triangle

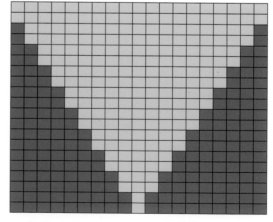

Small triangle is 19 stitches x 20 rows. Place in garment when front measures 7 (8, 9)". On wrong side row, work across row as est until 18 (19, 20) stitches remain on needle. Work in Color B to begin row 1 of Graph #3.

Triangle Treat Jumper

Designed to be worn over a blouse, this little jumper is soft and drapes beautifully. Complete it with the coordinating sweater on page 59 and your little "cheerleader" comes to life.

Triangle Treat Jumper

This pattern is sized 2T (3T, 4T).

●

FINISHED MEASUREMENTS
Total Length: 15 (17½, 20)"

Hem to Waist: 8 (9, 10)"

Bib: 4 (4½, 5)"

Shoulder Strap: 8 (10, 12)"

2T (3T, 4T)

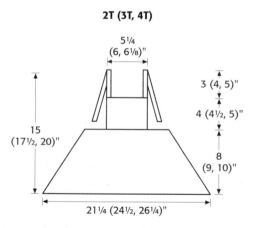

Materials

- Tahki Cotton Classic, 50-gram skeins (108 yds), 100% cotton (or any yarn that will meet the stitch gauge)
  Color A   3 (4, 4) skeins #3874 Blue
  Color B   2 (3, 3) skeins #3726 Lime Green
  Color C   2 (3, 3) skeins #3533 Yellow
- Size 6 needles: circular (24")
- 2 buttons
- Stitch holders

Gauge

22 sts and 28 rows = 4" in St st

To save time, always check your gauge. If necessary, change needle size to obtain correct gauge.

Pattern Stitch

TRIANGLE BORDER Design (see graph).

Skirt

USE CIRCULAR needles for this jumper, but work back and forth until you complete the graphed Triangle Border Design. In Color A, CO 234 (270, 288) sts.

> Rows 1–5: Purl.
>
> Row 6: Knit.
>
> Row 7: Purl.

On next row (RS), beg working the Triangle Border Design. After you have completed the design, join your work and beg knitting in the round, placing a st marker at the point of connection. K 2 rounds in Color A; K 2 rounds in Color C. Beg skirt shaping.

Skirt Shaping

In Color A, work as follows:

> Round 1: *K17, K2tog; repeat from * around.
>
> Rounds 2–4: Knit.
>
> Round 5: *K16, K2tog; repeat from * around.
>
> Rounds 6–8: Knit.
>
> Round 9: *K15, K2tog; repeat from * around.
>
> Rounds 10–12: Knit.
>
> Round 13: *K14, K2tog; repeat from * around.
>
> Rounds 14–16: Knit.

Round 17: *K13, K2tog; repeat from * around.

Rounds 18–20: Knit.

Round 21: *K12, K2tog, repeat from * around.

Rounds 22–24: Knit.

Round 25: *K11, K2tog; repeat from * around.

Rounds 26–28: Knit.

Round 29: *K10, K2tog; repeat from * around.

For sizes 3T and 4T only:

Rounds 30–32: Knit.

Round 33: *K9, K2tog; repeat from * around.

For all sizes:

Continue knitting in the round until skirt measures 8 (9, 10)" from beg.

Next round: Dec 12 (9, 12) sts evenly around until 118 (126, 132) sts rem.

Waist Ribbing

Rounds 1–5: K2, P2 across round to marker.

Rounds 6–8: Purl. At marker, est front and back bib sections as follows: BO 15 (15, 16) sts; place 29 (33, 34) sts on holder; BO 30 (30, 32) sts; place 29 (33, 34) sts on holder; BO 15 (15, 16) sts. Beg front bib section.

Front Bib Section

DISCONTINUE WORKING in the round. With RS facing, PU 29 (33, 34) sts from holder and work as follows: In Color A, P5 sts, K19 (23, 24) sts, P5 sts. Maintain the 5 purl sts in Color A on each edge for all rows. On the 19 (23, 24) center sts, follow color pattern in St st: *2 rows in Color A; 2 rows in Color C; 2 rows in Color A; 2 rows in Color B; repeat from * until center sts measure 4 (4½, 5)" from top of waistband. On next row, in Color A, purl all sts. For top edging, cont to purl for 4 rows. On next row, place 5 sts on holder; BO center sts; place 5 sts on holder.

Back Bib Section

WITH RS facing, PU and work the 29 (33, 34) sts on the 2nd st holder. Work back same as front, except work entire section in Color A, maintaining 5 purl sts for each edge and St st on the center sts. On Row 2 of the top edging, place a buttonhole (K2tog, yo) on each side, 3 sts in from each outside edge. For more information on buttonholes, see pages 16–18. Cont to purl for 3 rows. BO all stitches.

Shoulder Strap

PU 5 sts from holder on front bib section. Purl every row, cont until strap measures 8 (10, 12)". Repeat for second strap.

Finishing

SEW SIDE seam of Triangle Border Design. Sew a button on each shoulder strap. In Color A, single crochet a cord approx 36" long and weave evenly through waistband. Create 2 tassels (see page 27) and attach at each end of waistband tie.

The lime green and yellow colors alternate. Graph shows 36 stitches; continue working these 36 stitches around all stitches for Triangle Border Design.

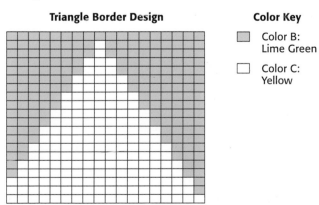

Triangle Border Design

Color Key

⬜ Color B: Lime Green

☐ Color C: Yellow

Sand Dune

"Sand Dune" is a unisex "tweener" cardigan in cotton that is perfect to take along to the beach or any-where. It consists of three multicolored, asymmetrical panels, which can present a knitting challenge.

If you are a beginning knitter, save this one until you have honed your knitting skills to an intermediate or advanced degree.

Sand Dune

This pattern is sized 18M (2T, 3T, 4T).

●

FINISHED MEASUREMENTS

Chest: 24 (26, 27, 28)"

Length: 11 (12, 13, 14)"

Drop Sleeve: 9 (10, 11, 12)"

18M (2T, 3T, 4T)

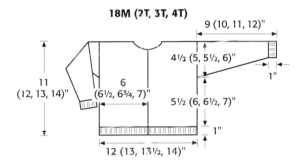

Materials

- Tahki Cotton Classic, 50-gram skeins (108 yds), 100% cotton
  Color A   1 (1, 1, 2) skeins #3407 Rust
  Color B   2 (2, 3, 4) skeins #3356 Gold
  Color C   1 (1, 1, 1) skein #3331 Brown
  Color D   1 (1, 1, 1) skein #3609 Green
- Size 6 needles: circular (24" and 16") or straight
- 5 (5, 6, 6) buttons (buttons shown are from Trendsetter Yarns)
- Stitch holders
- Stitch markers

Gauge

22 stitches and 28 rows = 4" in pattern stitch

To save time, always check your gauge. If necessary, change needle size to obtain correct gauge.

Pattern Stitch

Seed Stitch

Row 1 (RS): K1, P1 across row.

Row 2 (WS): Purl the knit sts and knit the purl sts.

Repeat Rows 1 and 2.

Back

THIS SWEATER is not knitted in the round, but you can use circular needles if you wish. In Color A, CO 66 (72, 74, 76) sts.

Rows 1–7: Work in K2, P2 ribbing.

Row 8 (RS): There are 3 panels on both the front and back of this sweater. Panel #1 is for the right side of the garment. Panel #2 is the center panel, which consists of working Rows 8 and 9 throughout garment. Panel #3 is for the left side of the garment. Est the number of sts in each panel as follows: For Panel #1, in Color C, K20 (22, 22, 22) sts. For Panel #2, in Color D, K3 sts; in Color B, work in seed st for 20 (22, 24, 26) sts; in Color D, K3 sts. For Panel #3, in Color A, K20 (22, 22, 22) sts.

Row 9: In Color A, P20 (22, 22, 22) sts; in Color D, P3 sts; in Color B, work in seed st for 20 (22, 24, 26) sts; in Color D, P3 sts; in Color C, P20 (22, 22, 22) sts.

Color Change Design for Panels #1 and #3

Row 1 (RS): In St st, *K2 in the color just completed, K2 in next color; repeat from * to end of row.

Row 2 (WS): Purl sts, repeating colors, as in Row 1.

Rows 3–4: Reverse colors and repeat the 2-st alternating color patt of Rows 1 and 2.

Cont to work sts and colors in panels as est, until garment measures 9 (11, 12, 13)". If necessary, cont in last panel color until measurement is reached. Beg back neck and shoulder shaping.

> **Panel #1: Right Side**
> Color C: work 10 (12, 14, 16) rows.
> Color Change Design: Work 4 rows.
> Color A: Work 32 (36, 40, 42) rows.
> Color Change Design: Work 4 rows.
> Color D: Work 20 (22, 24, 26) rows.
>
> **Panel #3: Left Side**
> Color A: Work 20 (22, 24, 26) rows.
> Color Change Design: Work 4 rows.
> Color D: Work 14 (16, 18, 20) rows.
> Color Change Design: Work 4 rows.
> Color B: Work 10 (12, 14, 14) rows.
> Color Change Design: Work 4 rows.
> Color C: Work 14 (16, 18, 20) rows.

Back Neck and Shoulder Shaping

On RS row, work patt on 23 (25, 25, 25) sts; place 20 (22, 24, 26) sts on holder; attach yarn and cont on 23 (25, 25, 25) sts. For shoulders, cont in est patt, dec 1 st at each neck edge EOR 3x. When garment measures 10 (12, 13, 14)", BO shoulder sts or place on st holder for seam method of preference.

Left Front

Rows 1–7: In Color A, CO 34 (36, 38, 40) sts. Work in K2, P2 ribbing.

Row 8 (RS): Note: left front Panel #3 is worked to correspond to back Panel #3, to which it is attached. In Color A, K20 (22, 22, 22) sts for Panel #3. For Panel #2, in Color D, K3 sts; in Color B, work 11 (11, 13, 15) sts in seed st.

Row 9 (WS): For Panel #2, in Color B, work 11 (11, 13, 15) sts in seed st; in Color D, P3 sts. For Panel #3, in Color A, P20 (22, 22, 22) sts. Staying in colors and sts as est, cont until left front measures 8½ (10½, 11, 12)". End with a RS row. Beg left front neck and shoulder shaping.

Left Front Neck and Shoulder Shaping

At neck edge (WS), BO 10 (10, 12, 12) sts, cont on rem 24 (26, 26, 28) sts in patt. For shoulder shaping, dec 1 st at neck edge EOR 4 (4, 4, 6)x. Work in panel patt until garment measures 10 (12, 13, 14)". BO shoulder sts or place on st holder for seam method of preference.

Right Front

Rows 1–7: For Panel #1, in Color A, CO 34 (36, 38, 40) sts. Work in K2, P2 ribbing for 7 rows. Right front is worked in Panel #1 and Panel #2 combination of 3 sts in Color D and seed st in Color B as follows:

Row 8 (RS): For Panel #2, in Color B, work 11 (11, 12, 13, 15) sts in seed st; in Color D, K3 sts. For Panel #1, in Color C, K20 (22, 22, 22) sts.

Row 9 (WS): For Panel #1, in Color C, P20 (22, 22, 22) sts. For Panel #2, in Color D, P3 sts; in Color B, work 11 (11, 13, 15) sts in seed st. Staying in colors and sts as est, cont until right front measures 8½ (10½, 11, 12)". Beg right front neck and shoulder shaping.

Right Front Neck and Shoulder Shaping

REVERSE SHAPING as for left front and work in patt until right front measures 10 (12, 13, 14)". BO shoulder sts or place on st holder for seam method of preference. Join shoulder seams.

Sleeves

THE SLEEVES are knitted from the top down. They are not knitted in the round, but you can use circular needles if you wish. Beg 4½ (5, 5½, 6)" from shoulder seam, mark back and front distance from shoulder before picking up sleeve sts. With RS facing, beg at one marker in Color B, PU 50 (55, 60, 66) sts, dividing sts evenly between front and back markers. Cont in Color B, in St st, until sleeve measures 5 (5, 6, 6)". Next RS row, work 6 rows of color striping as follows: 2 rows in Color C, 2 rows in Color D, 2 rows in Color A. Next row, in Color B, beg dec 1 st at each edge every fourth row 3 (5, 5, 7)x. Cont in St st until sleeve measures 8 (9, 10, 11)". In last row, dec 8 (7, 8, 8) sts evenly across row. In Color A, K2, P2 ribbing on rem 36 (38, 42, 44) sts for 6 rows. BO cuff loosely.

Neck Ribbing

WITH RS of garment facing, in Color A, PU 86 (90, 94, 98) sts around neck, including back sts on holder. Row 1 (WS): P2, K2 across row. Row 2 (RS): K2, P2 across row. Rows 3–4: Repeat Rows 1 and 2. Rows 5–9: Work 7 rows in St st. BO loosely.

Button Band

WITH RS of work facing, in Color A, PU 52 (62, 66, 70) sts along left front edge (not on neck ribbing). Work in K2, P2 ribbing for 7 rows. BO. Repeat for right front, placing 5 (5, 6, 6) buttonholes in fourth row (K2tog, yo) evenly on band. For more information on buttonholes, see pages 16–18. Garment as shown displays only 2 buttonholes with oversized decorative buttons.

Finishing

JOIN SLEEVE and side seams. Sew on buttons to correspond with buttonholes.

A stylish complement to any wardrobe, this cardigan
has a high waistband, giving it a retro look. It is
wonderful in any color.

Warm 'n Woolly

This pattern is sized 2T (4T, 6).

●

FINISHED MEASUREMENTS

Chest: 26 (28, 30)"

Length: 12 (14, 16)"

Sleeve: 10 (12, 14)"

2T (4T, 6)

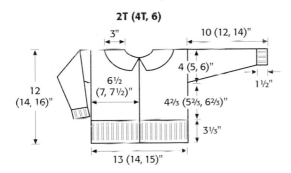

Materials

- Cascade Yarn's 220, 100-gram skeins (220 yds), 100% wool
  Color A 9322   2 (3, 4) skeins Green
  Color B 8884   1 (1, 1) skein Red
- Size 8 needles: circular (24") (for body)
- Size 10½ needles: circular (24") (for collar)
- Stitch holders
- Large-eyed sewing needle
- 5 buttons (buttons shown are JHB)

Gauge

18 stitches and 24 rows = 4" in pattern stitch

To save time, always check your gauge. If necessary, change needle size to obtain correct gauge.

Pattern Stitch

Seed Stitch

Row 1 (RS): K1, P1 across row.

Row 2 (WS): Purl the knit sts and knit the purl sts.

Repeat Rows 1 and 2.

Front and Back

THIS SWEATER is knitted on circular needles, but it is not knitted in the round. In Color A, CO 104 (126, 136) sts.

Rows 1–20: Work back and forth on the needles in a K2, P2 ribbing. When ribbing measures 3 (3½, 4)", beg sweater body.

Sweater Body

Row 1: In Color A, knit across.

Row 2: Purl across.

Row 3: In Color B, knit across.

Row 4: *K1, P1; repeat from * across row.

Row 5: K2, P1; knit across until last 3 sts; then P1, K2.

Row 6: P2, K1; purl across until last 3 sts; then K1, P2.

Continue repeating Rows 5 and 6 until front measures 8 (9, 10)". At this point, create armholes by dividing sts into 3 sections. Each front section should be 26 (31, 34) sts, and the back section 52 (64, 68) sts. Place back sts on a st holder. Working with front sts, cont in St st until front sections measure 10 (12, 14)". Beg neck shaping.

Front Neck Shaping

BO FIRST 8 (10, 12) sts at each neck edge. Cont in patt st, dec 1 st every row at neck edge 4x. Work rem 14 (15, 18) sts until each front piece measures 12 (14, 16)". BO shoulder sts or place on st holder for seam method of preference.

Back Neck Shaping

PICKING UP sts from st holder, cont working in Color A until back measures 12 (14, 16)". BO the 14 (17, 18) shoulder sts or place on st holder for seam method of preference. Place rem neck sts back on holder until the collar is knitted. Join shoulder seams.

Sleeves

THE SLEEVES are knitted from the top down. They are not knitted in the round, but you can use circular needles if you wish. With RS facing, in Color A, PU 46 (50, 54) sts evenly around opening. Work in St st until sleeve measures 8 (10, 12)". On next row, dec 10 (12, 14) sts evenly across row. Work final 10 rows in K2, P2 ribbing. BO in K2, P2 for cuff.

Collar

ON SIZE 10½ circular needles and with WS of garment facing, in Color B, PU 60 (68, 76) sts, including the sts from st holders. Work with 2 strands of Color B in seed st patt until collar measures 3" or desired length. BO loosely in K1, P1.

Button Band

WITH RS facing in Color A, PU 45 (54, 63) sts along the left front edge of sweater. Work 5 rows of K1, P1 seed st. BO in K1, P1. Repeat, picking up the same number of sts along right front edge. Working 5 rows in K1, P1 seed st, create 5 buttonholes evenly spaced along right front band. For more information on buttonholes, see pages 16–18. BO in K1, P1.

Finishing

SEW SLEEVE seams tog. Stitch buttons to left button band.

Don't you love bright colors? Children certainly do. To economize on your yarn purchase, knit this cardigan for that special little girl and make "Jazzy Juggler" for your favorite little guy. Both use the same yarn in the same colors.

Circus Parade

This pattern is sized: 18M (2T, 4T, 6).

●

FINISHED MEASUREMENTS

Chest: 24 (26, 28, 30)"

Length: 13 (14, 15, 16)"

Sleeve: 9 (10, 12, 14)"

18M (2T, 4T, 6)

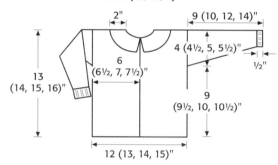

Materials

- Tahki Cotton Classic, 50-gram skeins (108 yds), 100% cotton

Color A 3002	1 (1, 1, 1) skein	Black
Color B 3997	2 (2, 2, 3) skeins	Red
Color C 3553	1 (1, 2, 2) skeins	Yellow
Color D 3764	1 (2, 2, 2) skeins	Green
Color E 3459	2 (2, 2, 2) skeins	Pink
Color F 3873	1 (2, 2, 2) skeins Royal Blue	
Color G 3001	1 (1, 1, 1) skein	White

- Size 6 needles: circular (24") or straight

- Stitch holders
- 6 multicolored buttons (buttons shown are JHB)

Gauge

22 stitches and 20 rows = 4" in pattern stitch

To save time, always check your gauge. If necessary, change needle size to obtain correct gauge.

Pattern Stitch

Seed Stitch

Row 1 (RS): K1, P1 across row.

Row 2 (WS): Purl the knit sts and knit the purl sts.

Repeat Rows 1 and 2.

Front and Back

THIS GARMENT is not knitted in the round, but you can use circular needles if you wish. In Color A, CO 134 (144, 154, 164) sts.

Rows 1–2: Work garter st (knit every row) in Color A.

Rows 3–8: Using Colors A and G, create a 2-st, 2-row checkerboard patt.

Row 9: In Color A, knit across row.

Rows 10–24: Working St st in Colors C and B, create the Heart design, following the graph.

Rows 25–26: Work St st in Color E.

Row 27: Beg color block pattern: Work right front 33 (36, 38, 41) sts in Color F. Work back 68 (72, 78, 82) sts in Color B. Work left front 33 (36, 38, 41) sts in Color D. Cont in St st patt until sweater measures 9 (9½, 10, 10½)". Divide at color block changes to create armholes. Place back sts on st holder. Working with front sections, cont in St st until front measures 11 (12, 13, 14)". Beg front neck shaping.

Front Neck Shaping

BO FIRST 8 (10, 12, 14) sts at each neck edge. Cont working in color patt, dec 1 st at each neck edge every row 6x. When front measures 13 (14, 15, 16)", BO shoulder sts or place on st holder for seam method of preference.

Back

PU BACK sts from st holder. Work St st in Color B until back measures 13 (14, 15, 16)". BO the 19 (20, 20, 21) shoulders sts or place them on a st holder for seam method of preference. Place center sts on st holder. Join shoulder seams.

Button Band

LEFT BUTTON band: With RS facing, in Color G, PU 60 (66, 70, 76) sts along left front. Work in seed st for 5 rows. BO in K1, P1. Right button band: In Color C, PU the same number of sts and work as for left button band, creating 6 buttonholes evenly spaced down button band. For more information on buttonholes, see pages 16–18. BO in K1, P1.

Collar

WITH WS of garment facing, in Color A, PU 80 (90, 100, 105) sts, including those on st holders. Work 12 rows in seed st. BO loosely.

Sleeves

THE SLEEVES are knitted from the top down. They are not knitted in the round, but you can use circular needles if you wish. With RS facing, in Color E, PU 44 (50, 55, 60) sts. Work in St st, except for every tenth row, which is worked in K1, P1

across, until sleeve measures 6½ (7½, 9½, 11½)". On next row, dec 10 (12, 14, 16) sts evenly across row. Work final 3 rows of K1, P1 ribbing for cuff in Color A. BO in ribbing.

Finishing

SEW SLEEVE and side seams tog. In Color E, single crochet around sweater bottom, both button bands, and collar. Block sweater carefully. Sew buttons on button band. Tack collar down in front if desired.

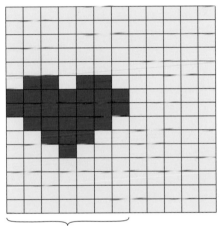

Heart Graph

1 heart

Heart design is 7 stitches x 6 rows.
Work graphed design in St st,
spacing as many hearts around sweater
as you wish.

Jazzy Juggler

The name says it all—your little one will want to wear this colorful tunic every day! Tassels around the hem add a festive touch. This pattern coordinates with "Circus Parade."

Jazzy Juggler

This pattern is sized 18M (2T, 4T, 6).

●

FINISHED MEASUREMENTS

Chest: 24 (26, 28, 30)"

Length (without fringe): 13 (14, 15, 16)"

Sleeve: 9 (10, 12, 14)"

18M (2T, 4T, 6)

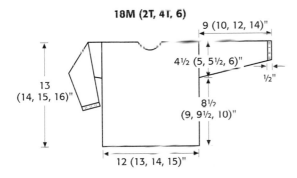

Materials

- Tahki Cotton Classic, 50-gram skeins (108 yds), 100% cotton

Color A 30021	(1, 1, 1) skein	Black
Color B 39471	(2, 2, 2) skeins	Purple
Color C 35531	(1, 1, 1) skein	Yellow
Color D 37641	(2, 2, 2) skeins	Green
Color E 34591	(1, 1, 1) skein	Pink
Color F 34011	(1, 1, 2) skeins	Orange
Color G 39971	(1, 1, 1) skein	Red
Color H 38731	(1, 1, 1) skein	Royal Blue
Color I 30011	(1, 1, 1) skein	White

- Size 6 needles: circular (24" and 16"). If desired, straight needles can be used for the sleeves.

- Stitch holders
- Stitch markers

Gauge

22 stitches and 28 rows = 4" in pattern stitch
To save time, always check your gauge. If necessary, change needle size to obtain correct gauge.

Front and Back

THIS GARMENT is knitted in the round. In Color A, CO 134 (144, 154, 164) sts.

Rounds 1–3: In Color A, purl around.

Rounds 4–6: In Color C, knit around.

Round 7: In Color D, K1, P1 around.

Round 8: In Color D, knit around.

Round 9: *In Color E, K1; in Color D, K3; repeat from * around.

Round 10: *In Color E, K3; in Color D, K1; repeat from * around.

Round 11: In Color E, knit around.

Round 12: *In Color E, K1; in Color H, K3; repeat from * around.

Round 13: In Color H, knit around.

Round 14: In Color H, *K3, P1, repeat from * around.

Rounds 15–17: In Color H, knit around.

Round 18: *In Color D, K1; in Color H, K1; repeat from * around.

Rounds 19–20: In Color G, knit around.

Rounds 21–22: *In Color A, K2; in Color I, K2; repeat from * around.

Rounds 23–24: *In Color I, K2; in Color A, K2; repeat from * around.

Rounds 25–26: Repeat Rounds 21–22.

Rounds 27–28: In Color G, knit around.

Round 29: In Color C, K1, P1 around.

Rounds 30–31: In Color C, knit around.

Round 32: In Color F, knit around.

Divide sts into 2 sections for front and back. Place back sts on st holder. Place marker at center front of sweater. Working back and forth on the needle in St st, work right half of sweater front in Color B and left half of sweater front in Color D. At the same time, create a 17-st, 17-row diamond in Color E, following the Diamond Design graph on page 79. When the first diamond is finished, create a second diamond directly above the first one in Color C. Then create a third diamond above the other two in Color G. Next, work 2 rows (completely across front) in Color E. Switch to Color A and K1, P1 across row. Work in St st in Color A until sweater front measures 11½ (12½, 13, 14)". Beg front neck shaping.

Front Neck Shaping

WITH RS facing, work across 23 (25, 25, 27) sts for first shoulder; place center 21 (22, 27, 28) sts on a st holder; cont across second shoulder. Cont working in Color A, dec 1 st at each neck edge every row 5 (5, 6, 6)x. When front measures 13 (14, 15, 16)", BO shoulder sts or place on st holder for seam method of preference.

Back

PU BACK sts from st holder. In Color F, work in St st until back measures 13 (14, 15, 16)". BO shoulder sts or place on st holder for preferred seam method. Place center 31 (34, 39, 40) sts on holder. Join shoulder seams.

Rolled Neck Edging

WITH RS of garment facing, in Color A, PU 74 (78, 88, 92) sts, including those on st holders for neck edging. Work in St st for 7 rounds. BO loosely. Let collar roll out.

Sleeves

THE SLEEVES are knitted from the top down. They are not knitted in the round, but you can use circular needles if you wish. Beg 4½ (5, 5½, 6)" from shoulder seam, mark back and front distance before picking up sleeve sts. Right sleeve: With RS facing, in Color D, PU 50 (55, 60, 66) sts. Work in St st until sleeve measures 6½ (7½, 9½, 11½)". On next K row, *K1 in Color D, K1 in color H, repeat from * across row. Work 5 rows in Color H. On next row, *K1 in Color E, K3 in Color H, repeat from * across row. Work next 3 rows in Color E. On next row, *K1 in Color D, K3 in Color E, repeat from * across row. On next row, *K1 in Color E, K3 in Color D, repeat from * across row. Work 2 rows in Color D. On next row, in Color C, K1, P1 across row. On next row, in Color C, dec 10 (12, 14, 16) sts evenly across row. In Color A, work 4 rows of garter st (knit every row) for cuff. BO. Left sleeve: Work same as right sleeve, substituting Color B for the first section of Color D.

Finishing

SEW SLEEVE and side seams tog. Using all of the colors, make 6-strand tassels, looping them through the hem every inch. Trim tassels to desired length. Block sweater carefully.

Diamond Design

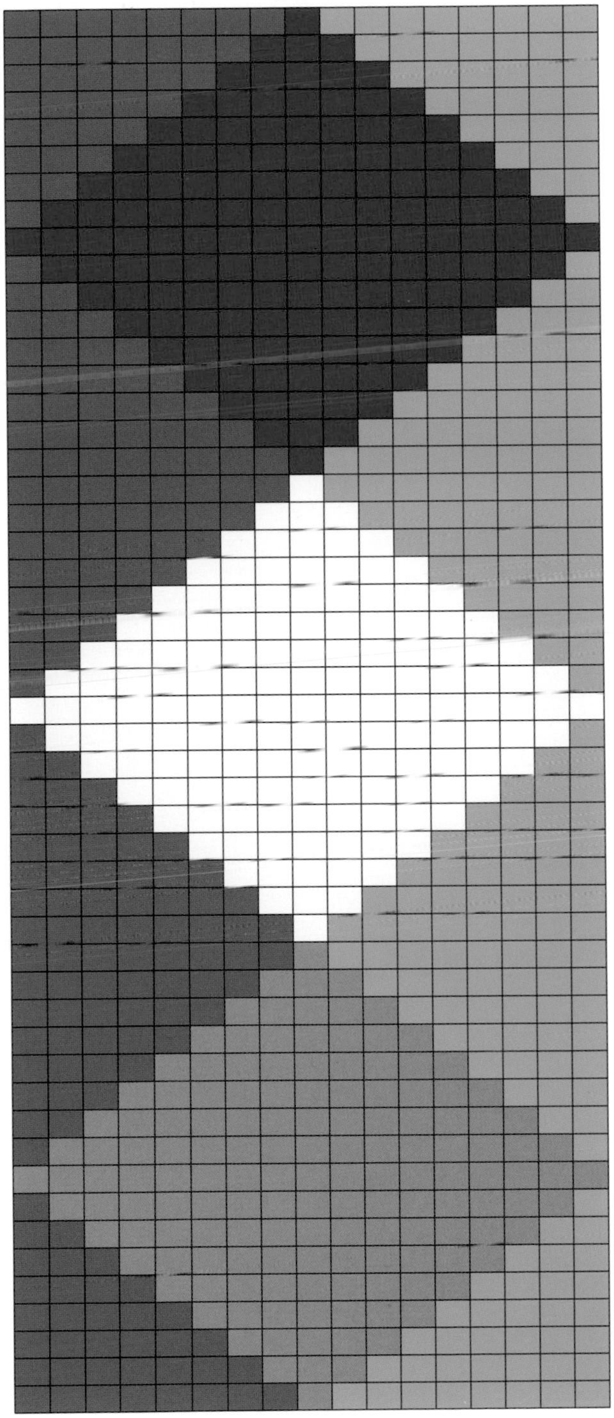

Color Key

- ■ Color B: Purple
- □ Color C: Yellow
- ■ Color D: Green
- ■ Color E: Pink
- ■ Color G: Red

Diamond design is 17 stitches x 17 rows.

Blue Daze

Cotton is the perfect yarn for this short-sleeved
sweater. After spending a long day in the garden, we
designed this tunic for one of our own little girls.

Blue Daze

This pattern is sized 18M (2T, 4T).

●

FINISHED MEASUREMENTS

Chest: 22 (24, 27)"

Length: 13 (14, 15½)"

Sleeve: 2¾ (3, 3½)"

18M (2T, 4T)

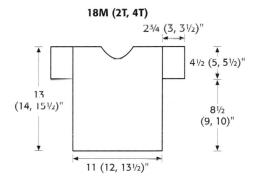

Materials

- Tahki Cotton Classic, 50-gram skeins (108 yds), 100% cotton
  Color A   2 (3, 3) skeins #3839 Blue
  Color B   2 (2, 2) skeins #3533 Yellow
  Color C   1 (1, 1) skein #3532 Light Yellow
  Color D   1 (1, 1) skein #3783 Teal
- Size 6 needles: circular (24" and 16") or straight
- Stitch holders

Gauge

22 stitches and 28 rows = 4" in pattern stitch
To save time, always check your gauge. If necessary, change needle size to obtain correct gauge.

Pattern Stitch

SEE FLOWER Design graph on page 82.

Garter Stitch

Knit every row.

Front

THIS SWEATER is not knitted in the round, but you can use circular needles if you wish. In Color A, CO 60 (65, 73) sts.

Rows 1–3: Knit in garter st.

On next row, with RS facing, beg working in St st as follows: 2 rows in Color A, 4 rows in Color B, 2 rows in Color C, 1 row in Color A, 3 rows in Color B, 8 rows in Color A.

On next row, K2 sts in Color B; K2 sts in Color A; repeat across row. Working in Color B, cont in St st for 5 rows. Follow Flower Design graph on page 82 for flower pattern. Place 3 flowers evenly across front. When Flower Design is complete, work 9 rows in Color B. On next row, repeat K2 sts in Color B, K2 sts in Color A across row. Work 8 rows in Color A, 5 rows in Color C, 3 rows in Color B, 1 row in Color A, 2 rows in Color C, and 5 (8, 12) rows in Color A. Beg front neck shaping.

Front Neck Shaping

ON NEXT row, work 22 (24, 26) sts; place next 16 (17, 21) sts on st holder; attach second ball of yarn and work rem 22 (24, 26) sts. Working shoulders at same time, cont in St st, dec 1 st every row at each neck edge 5 (6, 7)x. Work rem 17 (18, 19) sts until front measures 13 (14, 15½)". BO shoulder sts or place on st holder for seam method of preference.

Back

REPEAT AS for front to neck shaping. Cont in Color A until back measures 13 (14, 15½)". Beg back neck shaping.

Back Neck Shaping

BO THE 17 (18, 19) shoulder sts and sew shoulder seams tog or place sts on a st holder and knit the shoulder sts tog. Place the center 26 (29, 35) sts on holder.

Sleeves

THE SLEEVES are knitted from the top down. They are not knitted in the round, but you can use circular needles if you wish. Measure 4½ (5, 5½)" from shoulder seam in both directions and insert a st marker. With RS facing, PU 50 (55, 60) sts evenly between st markers. In Color A, work in St st until sleeve measures 2½ (2¾, 3¼)". On next row, K2tog every 5 sts. On rem sts, work 3 rows of garter st. BO loosely for cuff.

Neck Edge

USING 16" circular needles and with RS of garment facing, in Color A, PU 72 (80, 98) sts for neck edging. Purl 1 round; knit 1 round; purl 1 round. BO edging.

Finishing

IN COLOR C, make French knots in each flower center. Sew side seams and sleeve seams tog. Single crochet in Color C at neck edge, sleeve cuff, and bottom edge of garment for finished edging.

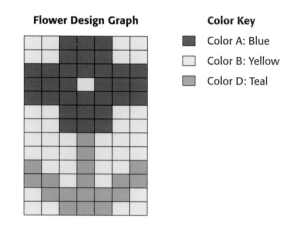

Flower Design Graph

Color Key
- Color A: Blue
- Color B: Yellow
- Color D: Teal

Flower design is 7 stitches x 13 rows.

Blue Lagoon

Here's an easier version of the traditional argyle design. Working in the round makes these diamonds a snap to knit. And by loosely trailing the yarn behind your work, you have no ends to weave in!

Blue Lagoon

This pattern is sized 18M (2T, 3T, 4T).

●

FINISHED MEASUREMENTS

Chest: 24 (26, 28, 30)"

Length: 13 (14, 15, 16)"

Sleeve: 2½ (3, 3, 3½)"

18M (2T, 3T, 4T)

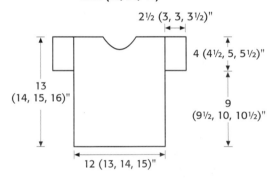

Materials

- Tahki Cotton Classic, 50-gram skeins (108 yds), 100% cotton

  Color A 3808 2 (2, 3, 3) skeins Aquamarine

  Color B 3873 2 (2, 2, 3) skeins Royal Blue

  Color C 3764 2 (2, 2, 2) skeins Kelly Green

- Size 6 needles: circular (24" and 16"). If desired, straight needles can be used for the sleeves.

- Size G crochet hook
- Stitch holders

Gauge

22 stitches and 28 rows = 4" in pattern stitch
To save time, always check your gauge. If necessary, change needle size to obtain correct gauge.

Front and Back

THIS SWEATER is knitted in the round. In Color B, CO 132 (144, 156, 168) sts.

> Rounds 1–2: Purl.
>
> Round 3: Knit.

Work Blue Lagoon Diamond design, referring to the graph on page 85. When garment measures 9 (9½, 10, 10½)", divide into 2 sections for front and back. Place back sts on a holder. Working back and forth on the front sts, cont in patt until front measures 11½ (12½, 13, 14)". Beg front neck shaping.

Front Neck Shaping

WITH RS facing, work across 23 (25, 27, 29) shoulder sts; place center 20 (22, 24, 26) sts on a st holder; cont across 2nd shoulder. Working both shoulders in patt, dec 1 st at each neck edge every row 6 (6, 7, 7)x until front measures 13 (14, 15, 16)". BO shoulder sts or place on st holder for seam method of preference.

Back

PICK UP back sts from holder and work back the same as front, omitting front neck shaping until garment measures 13 (14, 15, 16)". BO shoulder sts or place on st holder for seam method of preference. Place 32 (34, 38, 40) sts on holder. Join shoulder seams.

Neck Edging

WITH RS of garment facing, in Color B, PU 72 (76, 78, 84) sts around neck opening, including those sts on holders. Work in K1, P1 for 1 round. BO neck edge.

Sleeves

THE SLEEVES are knitted from the top down. They are not knitted in the round, but you can use circular needles if you wish. With RS facing, in Color A, PU 50 (56, 60, 66) sts evenly around opening. Work in St st until sleeve measures 2 (2½, 2½, 3)". On next row, dec 10 (12, 14, 16) sts evenly across row. Work 3 rows of K1, P1 for cuff. BO.

Finishing

SEW SLEEVE seams tog. Single crochet around hem, neck edging, and sleeve cuffs. Block carefully.

Blue Lagoon Diamond

Color Key
- Color A: Aquamarine
- Color B: Royal Blue
- Color C: Kelly Green

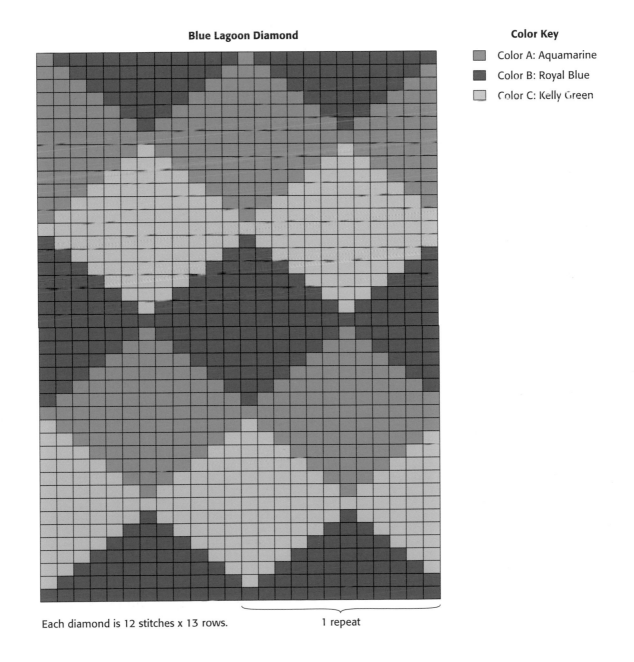

Each diamond is 12 stitches x 13 rows.

1 repeat

Sassy Sundress

Bright and colorful, this little sundress is the perfect summer statement. Worked in a cotton yarn, it would be great for your little girl's next birthday party.

Sassy Sundress

This pattern is sized 18M (2T, 3T, 4T).

●

FINISHED MEASUREMENTS

Front bib width: 6½ (7¼, 7¼, 8)"

Total Length: 14 (15½, 17½, 19)"

Hem to Waist: 7 (8, 9, 10)"

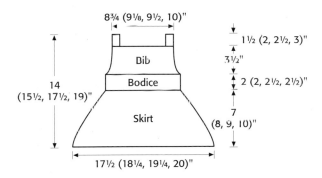

18M (2T, 3T, 4T)
Front

8¾ (9⅛, 9½, 10)"

1½ (2, 2½, 3)"

3½"

Bib

Bodice

2 (2, 2½, 2½)"

14
(15½, 17½, 19)"

Skirt

7
(8, 9, 10)"

17½ (18¼, 19¼, 20)"

Back

5 (5½, 6, 6½)"

4½"

Bodice

2 (2, 2½, 2½)"

14
(15½, 17½, 19)"

Skirt

7
(8, 9, 10)"

Materials

- Tahki Cotton Classic, 50-gram skeins (108 yds), 100% cotton
  Color A   2 (3, 3, 4) skeins #3459 Raspberry
  Color B   1 (1, 1, 1) skein #3726 Green
  Color C   1 (1, 1, 1) skein #3533 Yellow
- Size 6 needles: circular (24"). If desired, straight needles can be used for the bodice.
- 6 buttons
- Stitch holders
- Stitch markers

Gauge

22 stitches and 28 rows = 4" in pattern stitches
To save time, always check your gauge. If necessary, change needle size to obtain correct gauge.

Pattern Stitches

Double Seed Stitch for Sizes 2T and 3T (multiple of 4 stitches)

> Row 1: *K2, P2; repeat from * across.
>
> Row 2: As the sts face you, knit the knit sts and purl the purl sts.
>
> Row 3: As the sts face you, knit the purl sts and purl the knit sts.
>
> Row 4: As the sts face you, knit the knit sts and purl the purl sts.
>
> Rows 5–8: Repeat Rows 1–4.

Double Seed Stitch for Sizes 18M and 4T (multiple of 4 stitches plus 2)

> Row 1: *K2, P2; repeat from* to last 2 sts, end K2.

Rows 2–4: Follow Rows 2-4 as given above for sizes 2T and 3T.

Rows 5–8: Repeat Rows 1–4, ending with K2.

Skirt

THE SKIRT is knitted in the round. In Color B, CO 192 (200, 212, 220) sts. Join ends without twisting sts and place marker at point of connection. Round 1: K2, P2 around. Round 2: in Color A, K2, P2 around. Rounds 3–4: P2, K2 around. Rounds 5–6: K2, P2 around. Round 7: knit all sts. Round 8: in Color B, knit all sts. Round 9: in Color C, knit all sts. Rounds 10–11: K2, P2 around. Rounds 12–13: P2, K2 around. Rounds 14–15: K2, P2 around. Rounds 16–17: in Color B, knit all sts. Round 18: in Color A, knit all sts, dec 2 (0, 2, 0) sts, evenly spaced, until 190 (200, 210, 220) sts rem. Knit all rounds even until garment measures 6 (7, 8, 9)".

Waist Shaping

BEG DEC at marker as follows: Round 1: *K3, K2tog twice, K3; repeat from * to marker. Round 2: knit all sts. Round 3: *K3, K2tog, K3; repeat from * around. Round 4: knit all sts. Round 5: *K2, K2tog, K3; repeat from * around. Round 6: knit all sts. Round 7: *K2, K2tog, K2; repeat from * around. Round 8: knit all sts. There are 95 (100, 105, 110) sts on needle; garment should measure 7 (8, 9, 10)".

Front Bodice

THE BODICE is not knitted in the round, but you can use circular needles if you wish. Divide front and back sections: 49 (52, 53, 56) sts for front and 46 (48, 52, 54) sts for back. Work back and front sections separately. Place back bodice sts on st holder and proceed with front bodice. Row 1: In Color C (RS), knit across and dec 1 (0, 1, 0) st at end of row until 48 (52, 52, 56) sts rem. Rows 2–3: K2, P2

across row. Rows 4–5: P2, K2 across row. Rows 6–7: K2, P2 across row. Rows 8–9: P2, K2 across row. Rows 10–11 (for sizes 3T and 4T only): K2, P2 across row. Row 12 (all sizes): Purl. In Color B (RS), knit across row. On next row, work double seed st on 14 (16, 16, 16) sts, beg with K2; P20 (20, 20, 24) center sts; work double seed st on 14 (16, 16, 16) sts, beg with P2 (K2, K2, K2). On next row, work double seed st at edges and St st on center sts. Staying in Color B, on next row, work double seed st on 14 (16, 16, 16) sts; on center 20 (20, 20, 24) sts, beg stripe patt as follows: 2 rows in Color A, 2 rows in Color C, 2 rows in Color B; repeat as needed to obtain measurement; in Color B, work double seed st on 14 (16, 16, 16) sts. Stay in est patt until garment measures 9 (10, 11½, 12½)".

Front Armhole Shaping:

BO 4 sts at each armhole edge. Cont in est patt, dec 1 st at each edge every fourth row 2x until 8 (10, 10, 10) sts rem on either side of center section. Cont in patt until garment measures 11½ (12½, 14, 15)". Beg front neck shaping.

Front Neck Shaping

DISCONTINUE CENTER stripe pattern and work across all sts in double seed st, using Color B.

Work even in patt through sixth row. Row 7: Work 8 (10, 10, 10) sts in patt; BO center 20 (20, 20, 24) sts; work rem 8 (10, 10, 10) sts in patt. Cont on each shoulder strap in patt st until garment measures 14 (15½, 17, 19)" including strap. BO.

Back Bodice

PU 46 (48, 52, 54) sts from st holder.

Sizes 2T and 3T as follows:

In Color C, repeat instructions for front bodice through Row 9 for 2T and Row 11 for 3T.

In Color B:

Row 1: Knit.

Rows 2–3: K2, P2 across.

Rows 4–5: P2, K2 across. Stay in est. part until garment measures 9 (10, 11½, 12½)".

Sizes 18M and 4T as follows:

In Color C:

Row 1 (RS): Knit.

Row 2: K2, P2 across row, end K2.

Rows 3–4: P2, K2 across row, end P2.

Row 5: K2, P2 across row, end K2.

Repeat Rows 2–5 once more, then repeat Rows 2–3, 0 (1)x more. On next row, purl across. On next row, in Color B, knit across. *K2, P2 across row, end K2; P2, K2 across row, end P2; P2, K2 across row, end P2; K2, P2 across row, end K2; repeat from * as needed until piece measures 9 (10, 11½, 12½)".

Back Armhole Shaping

BO 4 sts at armhole edge; work rem 10 (12, 12, 12) sts in patt; join another skein of Color B and BO center 18 (16, 20, 22) sts; work 14 (16, 16, 16) sts in patt. On next row, BO 4 sts at armhole edge and work rem 10 (12, 12, 12) sts in patt. Working straps separately or at the same time with separate skeins attached to each strap, cont in patt st, dec 1 st at armhole edge every fourth row 2x. Staying in patt, work shoulder straps until garment measures 14 (15½, 17, 19)". BO. Join each strap at shoulder seam.

Back Bodice Side Button Tabs

BODICE BACK tabs lap over bodice front. In Color C, PU 14 (14, 16, 16) sts on each back from armhole edge to bottom row of Color C in waistband. Work in double seed st for 8 rows. At the same time, in fourth row, work 2 buttonholes (yo, K2tog), evenly spacing them on tab. For more information on buttonholes, see pages 16–18. BO all sts.

Back Crossing Tab

ON INSIDE edge of a shoulder strap, in center of back opening, PU 6 sts and work in double seed st for 3". At seampoint on opposite strap, PU 6 sts and work corresponding tab for 3", placing 2 buttonholes horizontally on last 1½" of tab at same point on opposite strap.

Finishing

SEW BUTTONS in place opposite buttonholes on side button tabs and under buttonholes on back crossing tab.

Hot Number!

What little gal wouldn't look glamorous in this bright
dress? We mixed a "tweedy" version of the same
coral color to give this dress some added sparkle.

Hot Number!

This pattern is sized 2T (4T, 6).

●

FINISHED MEASUREMENTS

Chest: 24 (26, 27½)"

Length: 17½ (19½, 21½)"

V-neck depth: 3 (3½, 4)"

2T (4T, 6)
(optional sleeve)

Materials

- Tahki Cotton Classic, 50-gram skeins (108 yds), 100% cotton
  Color A   4 (5, 5) skeins #3475 Coral
- Tweedy Cotton Classic, 50-gram skeins (108 yds), 100% cotton
  Color B   2 (2, 2) skeins #419 Coral for bodice without sleeves
            2 (3, 3) skeins #419 Coral for bodice with sleeves
- Size 6 needles: circular (24") or straight

- 6 (6, 7) buttons (buttons shown are JHB)
- Stitch holders
- Stitch markers

Gauge

22 stitches and 28 rows = 4" in pattern stitch
To save time, always check your gauge. If necessary, change needle size to obtain correct gauge.

Pattern Stitches

Skirt Ruffle Stitch (even number of stitches)

Row 1 (RS): K1, *yo, K2tog; repeat from *, ending K1.

Row 2 (WS): Purl.

Bodice Stitch

Row 1 (RS): *K4, P4; repeat from * across row.

Row 2 (WS): Work sts as presented, purling the purl sts and knitting the knit sts.

Rows 3–4: Repeat Rows 1–2.

Row 5 (RS): *P4, K4; repeat from * across row.

Rows 6–8: Repeat Rows 2–4.

Skirt

GARMENT IS worked in a back-and-forth manner with back and both front sections as one piece to armhole opening; do not work in the round. In Color A, CO 480 (528, 564) sts. Knit 1 row.

Rows 1–8: Work Rows 1 and 2 of skirt ruffle st 4x.

Row 9 (RS): P2tog across row until 240 (264, 282) sts rem.

Row 10 (WS): Knit across row, dec 1 (1, 0) st at midpoint.

Row 11 (RS): Est A-line panels as follows: K19 (21, 23), P1; *K39 (43, 46), P1; repeat from * 4x, ending K19 (21, 23).

Row 12 (WS): Purl all sts.

Rows 13–16: Repeat Rows 11–12.

Row 17 (RS): Staying in est A-line panel patt, beg A-line shaping. Knit to within 2 sts of the P1 st; work left slant dec (K2tog through back loop); work the P1 st; work right slant dec (K2tog through front loop) on next 2 sts; continue across row, working left and right slant dec on each side of the P1 st for a total dec of 12 sts in row. (Do not dec at front edge.)

On next row (WS), purl. Cont est patt, repeating Row 17 (A-line shaping) every eighth row 9 (10, 11)x until 131 (143, 130) sts rem. Work in patt until garment measures 11½ (12½, 14)" from beg. In last row of skirt, inc 1 (1, 0) st at midpoint in row. Beg bodice on next RS row.

Bodice

IN COLOR B, work Rows 1 and 2 in bodice st. Divide bodice sts between back and 2 front sections: Cont in patt with Row 3 of bodice st, work 32 (36, 38) sts and place on holder for right front; work 68 (72, 76) sts and leave on needle for back; place rem 32 (36, 38) sts on holder for left front.

Bodice Back

CONT WITH Row 4 of bodice st, work the 8-row pattern on back sts until garment measures 13 (15, 16½)" from beg. At the beg of the next 2 rows, BO 4 sts at armhole edge. Staying in est patt, dec 1 st at each armhole edge every row 2x. Cont until garment measures 17½ (19½, 21½)". On next row, BO 16 (17, 18) sts or place on st holder as preferred for first shoulder; place 24 (26, 28) sts on st holder

for neck, BO 16 (17, 18) sts or place on st holder as preferred for second shoulder.

Bodice Left Front

WITH RS facing, PU sts from holder. Attach yarn at armhole edge and beg with Row 3 of bodice st. Continue in 8-row patt until front measures 13 (15, 16½)" from beg. On next RS row, BO 4 sts, cont in bodice patt until left front measures 14 (15½, 17½)". Beg V-neckline shaping: At front neck edge, dec 1 st every row 12 (15, 16)x until 16 (17, 18) sts rem. Cont in patt until garment measures 17½ (19½, 21½)". BO sts as for back.

Bodice Right Front

WORK SAME as for left front except attach yarn at center front edge and beg with Row 4 of bodice st. Reverse armhole and neck shaping. Join shoulder seams.

Button Band

WITH RS of left front section facing, PU 68 (76, 84) sts along front edge, starting where V-neck shaping begins and ending at top of purl row before ruffle. Work Rows 1–4 of bodice st. BO loosely in patt. Right front button band is worked same as left front button band, except place 2 buttonholes in Rows 2–3 of bodice st in band, one within 2 sts of top and the other near base of bodice. For more information on buttonholes, see pages 16–18. For mock skirt opening, overlap and sew bands together below buttonholes.

Collar

BEG AT outside edge of button band with RS facing, PU 92 (96, 96) sts along neck edge, including sts on back st holder. K1, P1 for 3 rows. Work in Bodice st for 16 rows. BO loosely in patt.

Optional Sleeves

SLEEVES ARE knit from the top down. They are not knit in the round, but circular needles can be used if you wish. Beg 4 (4½, 5)" from shoulder seam, mark back and front distance before picking up sts. With RS facing, PU 44 (52, 60) sts. Purl WS return row. On next row, work 8-row bodice st; repeat until sleeve measures 3", ending with WS row. Border sleeves with 4 (4, 6) rows of skirt ruffle st. Purl 1 row. BO loosely.

Finishing

SEW SLEEVE seam (if applicable) and rem side opening tog. Space 6 (6, 7) buttons evenly down button band, placing 2 buttons on bodice to correspond with buttonholes. Block carefully.

Puddle Jumper

Have you ever found the shoes and then had to find a dress to match? That's what happened to us. The galoshes came first; then we designed a jumper to coordinate. It can be worn alone or with a T-shirt underneath.

Puddle Jumper

This pattern is sized 2T (3T, 4T).

●

FINISHED MEASUREMENTS
Chest: 20 (22, 24)"

Length: 16 (17, 18)"

2T (3T, 4T)

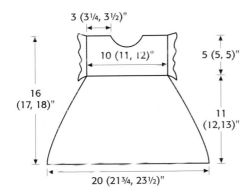

Materials

- Tahki Cotton Classic, 50-gram skeins (108 yds), 100% cotton

  Color A   3 (4, 4) skeins #3533 Yellow

  Color B   A small amount of #3001 White

  Color C   A small amount of #3764 Green
- Size 6 needles: circular (24")
- Stitch holders

- Size G crochet hook
- 3 buttons: 1 red, 1 blue, 1 green (model buttons are JHB)

Gauge

22 stitches and 28 rows = 4" in pattern stitch
To save time, always check your gauge. If necessary, change needle size to obtain correct gauge.

Pattern Stitch

Seed Stitch

Row 1 (RS): K1, P1 across row.

Row 2 (WS): Purl the knit sts and knit the purl sts.
Repeat Rows 1 and 2.

Jumper Skirt

SKIRT IS knitted in the round. In Color A, CO 220 (240, 260) sts.

Round 1: Purl.

Round 2: Purl.

Rounds 3–7: Knit.

Round 8: In Color C, K1, P1 around.

Round 9: In Color A, continue knitting rounds until skirt measures 11 (12, 13)".

Beg high-waist shaping: On next round, K2tog around. Work next 1" in seed st. Beg front bodice.

Front Bodice

ON NEXT round, divide sts into 2 sections for front and back. Place back sts on holder. Working back and forth on the front sts, cont in St st until garment measures 13 (14, 15)". Beg front neck shaping.

Front Neck Shaping

Work across 17 (18, 19) sts. BO center 21 (24, 27) sts. Attach second ball of yarn, work rem 17 (18, 19) sts. Dec 1 st at neck edge every row 3 x. Cont in patt until garment measures 16 (17, 18)". BO shoulders.

Back Bodice

PU BACK sts from holder; work same as front, omitting front neck shaping until garment measures 16 (17, 18)". BO all sts for shoulders and back of neck. Sew front and back shoulders tog.

Sleeve Ruffle

With RS facing, PU 24 sts (all sizes) at armhole edge for sleeve ruffle. On next row, inc 2 sts in each st across row. Beg working back and forth in a K4, P4 rib patt to create ruffle, knitting the knit sts and purling the purl sts for 2". BO in K4, P4.

Finishing

In Color B, single crochet around hem of skirt and neck opening. Sew buttons onto front of jumper along waistband with Color A. In Color B, single crochet 3 chains of 14 sts each. Loop each chain around a button and secure the loop above the button.

The floral border for this sundress was inspired by the wallpaper border in our new studio. Talk about an inspiring workplace! With this dress, we tied the shoulders with ribbon, which (in addition to being cute) allows a little growing room.

Petals

This pattern is sized 2T (3T, 4T).

●

FINISHED MEASUREMENTS

Chest: 20 (24, 26)"

Length: 16 (17, 18)"

2T (3T, 4T)

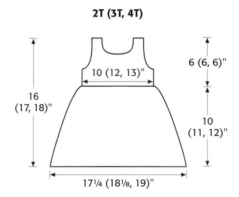

10 (12, 13)"

6 (6, 6)"

16 (17, 18)"

10 (11, 12)"

17¼ (18⅛, 19)"

Materials

- Tahki Cotton Classic, 50-gram skeins (108 yds), 100% cotton
  Color A   3 (3, 4) skeins #3839 Blue
  Color B   1 (2, 2) skeins #3001 White
  Color C   1 (1, 1) skein #3533 Yellow
  Color D   1 (1, 1) skein #3726 Green
- Size 6 needles: circular (24")
- Stitch holders
- 1½ yards of 1"-wide yellow ribbon
- Size G crochet hook

Gauge

22 stitches and 28 rows = 4" in pattern stitch

To save time, always check your gauge. If necessary, change needle size to obtain correct gauge.

Skirt

THE SKIRT is knitted in the round. In Color A, CO 190 (200, 210) sts.

> Round 1: Purl.
>
> Round 2: Purl.
>
> Rounds 3–7: Knit.
>
> Rounds 8–11: In Color C, knit.

Round 12: In Color D, K1, P1 around. Beg Petals Flower Design (see graph), taking care to knit 3 rounds of Color B both before and after graphed design. Place 19 (20, 21) flowers evenly around skirt. When flower design is complete, in Color C, K1, P1 around. Knit next 3 rounds. In Color A, cont knitting rounds until skirt measures 10 (11, 12)". Beg waist shaping: On next round, K2tog around. Work next row in a rib patt of *K3, P1; repeat from * around. Cont in patt for 2".

Bodice Front

ON NEXT round, divide sts into 2 sections for front and back bodice, placing the extra st, if needed, on back. Place back sts on holder. You will now be working back and forth on the needles. With RS facing, beg armhole shaping.

Armhole Shaping

BO 5 sts at each edge to create armholes. Cont working in rib patt, dec 1 st at each armhole edge 5x. Work front until garment measures 13 (14, 15)". Beg front neck shaping.

Front Neck Shaping

WORK ACROSS 8 (9, 10) sts in patt; BO center 11 (12, 12) sts; attach second ball of yarn and work rem 8 (9, 10) sts. Dec 1 st at neck edge every row, 3x. Cont in patt until garment measures 16 (17, 18)". BO shoulders.

Back Bodice

WORK SAME as front without front neck shaping until garment measures 14 (15, 16)". Beg back neck shaping.

Back Neck Shaping

ON NEXT row, work across 8 (9, 10) sts in patt; BO center 11 (12, 12) sts; attach second ball of yarn and work rem 8 (9, 10) sts. Dec 1 st at neck edge every row 3x. Cont in patt until garment measures 16 (17, 18)". BO shoulders.

Finishing

IN COLOR A, single crochet around hem of skirt, armholes, and neck opening. In Color A, single crochet a loop at the end of each shoulder strap. Pull length of ribbon through straps and tie in a bow on each shoulder.

Petals Flower Graph

Each flower is 9 stitches x 11 rows.

Sweet Petunia

Many little girls choose purple as their favorite color. With this in mind, we created this blooming sweet petunia dress. A wonderful, twisted cotton yarn gives it a lustrous sheen—perfect in any color for your favorite little petunia.

Sweet Petunia

This pattern is sized 18M (2T, 3T, 4T).

●

FINISHED MEASUREMENTS

Chest: 22 (24, 26, 28)"

Bodice Length: 6¹/₂ (7, 7¹/₂, 8)"

Total Dress Length: 15 (16, 17¹/₂, 19)"

Sleeve: 3 (3, 3¹/₂, 3¹/₂)"

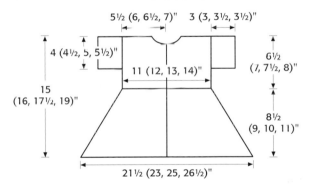

18M (2T, 3T, 4T)

5½ (6, 6½, 7)"   3 (3, 3½, 3½)"

4 (4½, 5, 5½)"

11 (12, 13, 14)"

6½ (7, 7½, 8)"

15 (16, 17½, 19)"

8½ (9, 10, 11)"

21½ (23, 25, 26½)"

Materials

- Cascade Yarn's Madil Cotton Cable, 50-gram skeins (123 yds), 100% combed cotton
  Color A   4 (5, 5, 6) skeins #557 Purple
  Color B   1 (1, 2, 2) skeins #558 Lilac
  Color C   1 (1, 1, 1) skein #562 Red
  Color D   1 (1, 1, 1) skein #565 Yellow
- Size 6 needles: circular (24") or straight
- Buttons 5 (6, 6, 7)
- Stitch holders

Gauge

23 stitches and 28 rows = 4" in pattern stitch

To save time, always check your gauge. If necessary, change needle size to obtain correct gauge.

Pattern Stitches

Seed Stitch

Row 1 (RS): K1, P1 across row.

Row 2 (WS): Purl the knit sts and knit the purl sts.

Repeat Rows 1 and 2.

Bodice Stitch

Row 1: In Color B, knit across row, inc 1 st in each st to double st count.

Rows 2, 4, 6: Purl across row.

Row 3: Knit all sts.

Row 5: K2tog across row to return to original st count.

Row 7: In Color A, knit across row.

Rows 8, 9, 10: In Color A, work in seed st (see below).

Dress Skirt

In Color A, CO 246 (266, 286, 306) sts. Dress is not knitted in the round, but you can use circular needles if you wish.

Row 1: To est seed st, K1, P1 across row.

Row 2: Knit the purl sts and purl the knit sts.

Rows 3–4: Repeat Rows 1 and 2.

Row 5: In Color B, work in seed st across row.

Row 6: Place 6 sts on holder; in Color A, knit across to last 6 sts, place rem 6 sts on holder. Rows 7–13: In Color A, work in St st.

Row 14 (color patt #1): K1 in Color A; *K2 in Color C, K8 in Color A; repeat from *; end K2 in Color C, K1 in Color A.

Rows 15–21: St st in Color A.

Row 22 (color patt #2): K2 in Color B; K4 in Color A; *K2 in Color B, K8 in Color A; repeat from * to last 8 sts; end K2 in Color B, K4 in Color A, K2 in Color B.

Cont as est, alternating 7 rows of St st in Color A with Row 14 (color patt #1) and Row 22 (color patt # 2). In Row 14, maintain accent color rotation of C, D, B and repeat from * as needed. In row 22, maintain accent color rotation of *B, C, D and repeat from * as needed. When garment measures 8½ (9, 10, 11)", beg waist dec: on next RS row, K2tog across row until 117 (127, 137, 147) sts rem.

Bodice

In COLOR A, work in seed st for 9 rows. Work in bodice st patt for 6 rows. In Row 7, divide sts into back and 2 front sections: work in patt on 26 (28, 32, 34) sts and place on st holder; leave 65 (71, 75, 79) sts on needle for bodice back; place rem 26 (28, 32, 34) sts on st holder. Working on bodice back, cont on Rows 8–10 of bodice st patt. At same time, for armhole shaping, BO 4 sts at beg of Rows 9 and 10 once. Repeat Rows 1–10 of bodice st patt 3 (3, 4, 4)x more. In Color A, work in seed st until garment measures 14½ (15½, 17, 18½)". On next row, work in seed st for 14 (15, 17, 18) sts for shoulder; place 29 (33, 33, 35) neck sts on st holder; attach second ball of yarn and work rem 14 (15, 17, 18) sts. Cont on shoulder sts until garment measures 15 (16, 17½, 19)". BO shoulder sts or place on st holder for seam method of preference.

Bodice Fronts

PU STS from st holders. In Color A, work in seed st for 9 rows. Work in bodice st patt for 8 rows. For armhole shaping, BO 4 sts at beg of ninth row for left front, and tenth row for right front. Repeat Rows 1–10 of bodice st patt 3 (3, 4, 4)x more. In Color A, work in seed st until garment measures 13½ (14, 15½, 16½)". At center front, BO 6 (7, 7, 8) sts; cont across row. Dec 1 st at neck edge FOR 2 (2, 3, 4)x. Cont on shoulder sts until garment measures 15 (16, 17½, 19)". BO shoulder sts or place on st holder for seam method of preference. Join shoulder seams.

Sleeves

THE SLEEVES are knitted from the top down. They are not knitted in the round, but you can use circular needles if you wish. Beg at edge of armhole BO with RS facing you, PU 54 (54, 64, 64) sts.

Rows 1–5: St st in Color A.

Row 6: Repeat Row 14 for skirt (color patt #1).

Rows 7–11: Repeat Rows 1–5.

Row 12: Repeat Row 22 for skirt (color patt #2). In Color A, work 5 (5, 7, 7) rows in St st. On next row, dec 12 (12, 16, 16) sts evenly across row. Work seed st border as follows: 2 rows in Color B; 1 (1, 2, 2) rows in Color C; 1 (1, 2, 2) rows in Color A. BO in Color A.

Button Band

PU 6 sts on left front and work in seed st to correspond with length of garment to top neck edge at BO. PU 6 sts on right front and work in same patt. Work 5 (6, 6, 7) buttonholes evenly along right button band, spacing bottom buttonhole approx 3" from bottom of garment, and top buttonhole within 3 rows of top. For more information on buttonholes, see pages 16–18.

Finishing

SEW SLEEVE seams. Sew button bands to front edge of garment. Single crochet in Color B around neck opening. Sew on buttons to correspond with buttonholes.

This sleek skirt and fitted bodice look great underneath the little ivory top that follows. In this ensemble, your little girl will be ready for high tea with the Queen of England!

Teatime Teal–Jumper

This pattern is sized 18M (2T, 3T, 4T).

●

FINISHED MEASUREMENTS

Chest: 17¼ (18, 19, 20)"

Total Length: 14 (15½, 17½, 19½)"

Hem to Waist: 7 (8, 9½, 10½)"

18M (2T, 3T, 4T)

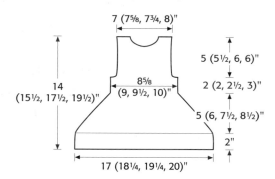

Materials

- Tahki Cotton Classic, 50-gram skeins (108 yds), 100% cotton
  Color A   3 (4, 5, 5) skeins #3786 Teal
- Size 6 needles: circular (24")
- 5 (5, 7, 7) buttons (buttons shown are JHB)
- Stitch markers

Gauge

22 sts and 28 rows = 4" in pattern stitches

To save time, always check your gauge. If necessary, change needle size to obtain correct gauge.

Pattern Stitches

Moss Stitch

Rows 1–2: *K1, P1; repeat from * across row.

Rows 3–4: *P1, K1; repeat from * across row.

Lace Ladder Stitch (multiple of 4 stitches)

Row 1 (RS): *ssk, (yo) twice, K2tog; repeat from *.

NOTE: "*(yo) twice*" *means to wrap yarn around needle 2x.*

Row 2: *P1, (P1, K1) into double yo, P1; repeat from *.

Repeat Rows 1 and 2.

Bodice Rib Pattern

Round 1: K2,*P1, K4, P1, K4; repeat from *; end K2 at marker.

Round 2: Knit.

When working back and forth in Rows: Round 2 becomes Row 2: Purl (WS).

Dress

SKIRT IS NOT knitted in the round until the beg of the St st section of the garment. In Color A, CO 192 (200, 212, 220) sts.

Row 1: Purl.

Rows 2–3: K1, P1 across.

Rows 4–5: P1, K1 across.

Rows 6–11: Work lace ladder st across row 3x.

Rows 12–13: K1, P1 across.

Rows 14–15: P1, K1 across.

Row 16: Beg St st in the round. Join sts without twisting, and mark for beg of next round.

Round 17: Knit all sts, dec 2 (0, 2, 0) sts, evenly spaced, across round until 190 (200, 210, 220) sts rem. Knit all rounds until garment measures 6 (7, 8, 9½)". Beg waist shaping.

Waist Shaping

Round 1: *K3, K2tog twice, K3; repeat from * to marker.

Round 2: Knit.

Round 3: *K3, P2tog, K3; repeat from * around.

Round 4: Knit.

Round 5: *K2, P2tog, K3; repeat from* around.

Round 6: Knit.

Round 7: *K2, P2 tog, K2; repeat from * around.

Round 8: Knit. There are 95 (100, 105, 110) sts rem.

NOTE: *Remainder of garment is worked from marker in rib patt as follows:*

Round 1: K2,*P1, K4, P1, K4; repeat from *, end K2 at marker.

Round 2: Knit.

Repeat Rounds 1 and 2 until garment measures 7 (8, 9, 10½)". Beg bodice front and discontinue working in the round.

Bodice Front

DIVIDE STS for front and back sections: leave 49 (52, 53, 56) sts on needle for front; place 46 (48, 52, 54) sts on st holder for back. Stay in 5-st rib patt (purl all WS sts). When garment measures 9 (10, 11½, 13½)", beg armhole shaping: BO 2 sts at each armhole edge. Cont in rib patt, dec 1 st EOR 3 (3, 3, 4)x. Beg front neck shaping.

Front Neck Shaping

WHEN GARMENT measures 12 (13, 15, 16½)", work 12 sts in patt; BO center 15 (18, 19, 20) sts; attach second ball of yarn and work rem 12 sts. Dec 1 st at neck edge EOR 2x. Cont in patt until garment measures 14 (15½, 17½, 19½)". BO shoulder sts or place on st holder for seam method of preference.

Back Bodice

PU THE 46 (48, 52, 54) back sts from st holder. Work same as for bodice front. At 9 (10, 11½, 12, 13½)", beg armhole shaping: BO 2 sts at each armhole edge. Dec 1 st EOR 2 (2, 2, 3)x. Cont until back bodice measures 10½ (11½, 13, 14½)". For neck placket, divide back sts into 2 sections to create back opening. Working separately, cont until each side measures 12 (13, 15, 16½)". At center opening, BO 7 (8, 10, 10) sts; work rem 12 sts. Dec 1 st at neck edge EOR row 2x. Work shoulders until garment measures 14 (15½, 17½, 19½)". BO shoulder sts or place on st holder for seam method of preference. Join shoulder seams.

Finishing

SIDE BUTTON tabs lap front over back bodice. For tabs, PU 12 (14, 16, 16) sts on each front side from armhole edge to skirt split. Work K1, P1 for 2 rows; P1, K1 for 2 rows; repeat last 4 rows. At the same time, in fourth row, work 2 (2, 3, 3) buttonholes (K2tog, yo), evenly spaced, on tab. For more information on buttonholes, see pages 16–18. Sew on buttons to correspond with buttonholes on side button tabs. Sew seam on skirt border. Single crochet around back neck opening, creating a 5-chain button loop, and attach button loop to top of back neck opening.

Teatime Teal-Top

This pattern is sized 18M (2T, 3T, 4T).

●

FINISHED MEASUREMENTS
Chest: 22 (23, 25, 26)"
Length: 7 (7, 9, 9)"

18M (2T, 3T, 4T)

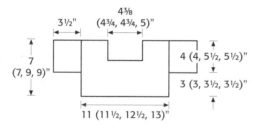

Materials

- Tahki Cotton Classic, 50-gram skeins (108 yds), 100% cotton
  Color B   2 (2, 3, 3) skeins #3003 Ecru
- Size 6 needles: circular (24") or straight
- 1 yd of 1/8" ecru satin ribbon

Gauge

22 sts and 28 rows = 4"

To save time, always check your gauge. If necessary, change needle size to obtain correct gauge.

Pattern Stitches

Moss Stitch

Rows 1–2: *K1, P1; repeat from * across row.

Rows 3–4: *P1, K1; repeat from * across row.

Lace Ladder Stitch (multiple of 4 stitches)

Row 1 (RS): *ssk, (yo) twice, K2tog; repeat from *.

NOTE: *"(yo) twice" means to wrap yarn around needle 2x.*

Row 2: *P1, (P1, K1) into double yo, P1; repeat from *.

Repeat Rows 1 and 2.

Front

THIS GARMENT is not knitted in the round, but you can use circular needles if you wish. In Color B, CO 60 (64, 72, 76) sts.

Row 1: Purl.

Rows 2–5: Work in moss st. Then, see lace ladder st.

Row 6 (RS): Begin lace ladder st in combination with moss st. (K1, P1) twice; *ssk, (yo) twice, K2tog; repeat from * 2 (2, 3, 3)x more; K1, P1 for 12 (12, 12, 16) sts; *ssk, (yo) twice, K2tog; repeat from * 2 (3, 3, 3)x more; *(K1, P1) twice; *ssk, (yo) twice, K2tog; repeat from * 2 (2, 3, 3)x more; (K1, P1) twice.

Row 7 (WS): (K1, P1) twice; *P1 (P1, K1) into double yo, P1; repeat from * 2 (2, 3, 3)x more; (K1, P1) twice; *P1 (P1, K1) into double yo, P1; repeat from * 2 (3, 3, 3)x more; K1, P1 for 12 (12, 12, 14) sts; *P1 (P1, K1) into double yo, P1; repeat from * 2 (2, 3, 3)x more; (K1, P1) twice.

Rows 8–11: Repeat Rows 6–7, keeping the K1, P1 sts in the moss st.

Rows 12–15: Work in moss st on all sts.

Row 16: Repeat the moss and lace ladder st combination in Rows 6–15 for 2 (2, 3, 3)x more. Total number of combinations at garment completion is 4 (4, 5, 5). At the same time, work armhole shaping.

Front and Back Armhole Shaping

WHEN GARMENT measures 3 (3, 3½, 3½)", BO 4 sts at armhole edge. Staying in patt, BO 1 st EOR 2 (2, 4, 4)x at each edge. After completing 3 (3, 4, 4) lace ladder and moss st combinations, beg neck shaping.

Front and Back Neck Shaping

ON NEXT row (RS), work 12 (13, 15, 16) sts in pattern; BO 24 (26, 26, 28) sts; work 12 (13, 15, 16) sts in patt (work separately or attach second ball of yarn and work at same time). Complete final repeat of moss and lace ladder st repetitions. Cont in moss st on shoulders until garment measures 7 (7, 9, 9)". BO shoulder sts or place on st holder for seam method of preference. Join shoulder seams.

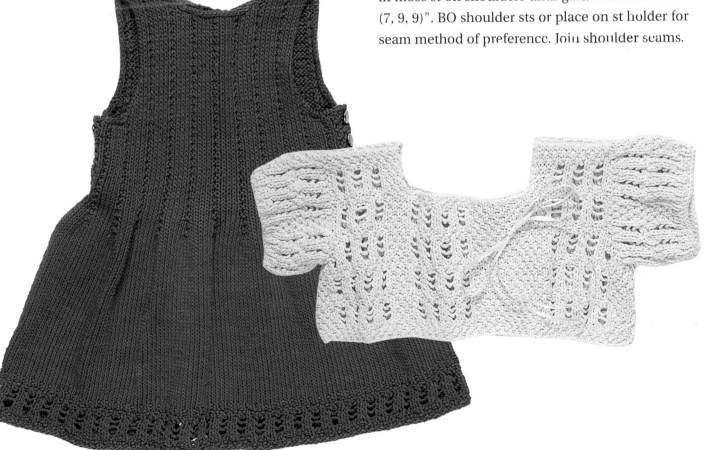

Back

CO 60 (64, 72, 76) sts.

Row 1. Purl.

Rows 2–5: Work in moss st.

Row 6 (RS): K1, P1 over 4 (2, 6, 4) sts; *ssk, (yo) twice, K2tog; repeat from * 1 (2, 2, 2)x more; (K1, P1) twice; *ssk (yo) twice, K2tog; repeat from * 2 (2, 2, 3)x more; (K1, P1) twice; *ssk, (yo) twice, K2tog; repeat from * 2 (2, 2, 3)x more; (K1, P1) twice; *ssk, (yo) twice, K2tog; repeat from * 1 (2, 2, 2)x more; K1, P1 over 4 (2, 6, 4) sts.

Row 7 (WS): K1, P1 over 4 (2, 6, 4) sts; *P1, (P1, K1) into double yo, P1; repeat from * 1 (2, 2, 2)x more; (K1, P1) twice; *P1 (P1, K1) into double yo, P1; repeat from * 2 (2, 2, 3)x more; (K1, P1) twice; *P1 (P1, K1) into double yo, P1; repeat from * 2 (2, 2, 3)x more; (K1, P1) twice; *P1 (P1, K1) into double yo, P1; repeat from * 1 (2, 2, 2)x more; K1, P1 over 4 (2, 6, 4) sts.

Rows 8–11: Repeat Rows 6–7, keeping the K1, P1 sts in the moss st patt.

Rows 12–15: Work in moss st on all sts.

Row 16: Repeat Rows 6–15 for 3 (3, 4, 4)x total. At the same time, work armhole and neck shaping.

Sleeves

THE SLEEVES are knitted from the top down. They are not knitted in the round, but you can use circular needles if you wish. With RS facing, PU 52 (52, 68, 68) sts around armhole edge.

Row 1: Purl.

Rows 2–5: Work in moss st.

Row 6: K1, P1 for 1 (1, 0, 0)x; work lace ladder st 3x; (K1, P1) twice; work lace ladder st 4x; (K1, P1) twice; work lace ladder st 3 (3, 4, 4)x; K1, P1 over 2 (2, 4, 4) sts; work lace ladder st 0 (0, 3, 3)x.

Row 7: Work lace ladder st 0 (0, 3, 3)x; K1, P1 over 2 (2, 4, 4) sts; work lace ladder st 3 (3, 4, 4)x; (K1, P1) twice; work lace ladder st 4x; (K1, P1) twice; work lace ladder st 3x; K1, P1 for 1 (1, 0, 0)x.

Rows 8–11: Repeat Rows 6–7.

Rows 12–15: Work in moss st.

Rows 16–21: Repeat Rows 6–7.

Rows 22–24: Work in moss st.

Row 25: BO in patt.

Finishing

SEW SLEEVE and side seams. Single crochet on neck and sleeve edges.

Winter Wonderland

With the holiday season in mind, we created a dress that can be worn all winter. This dress is so easy, and it fits like a charm. You will want to make this one again and again. Change the colors, create a border of your choice, and add a decorative button accent for another version of this sweet dress.

Winter Wonderland

This pattern is sized 18M (2T, 3T, 4T).

●

FINISHED MEASUREMENTS
Chest: 22 (24, 26, 28)"
Length: 15 (16, 17, 18)"
Sleeve: 2 1/4 (2 1/2, 2 3/4, 3)"

18M (2T, 3T, 4T)

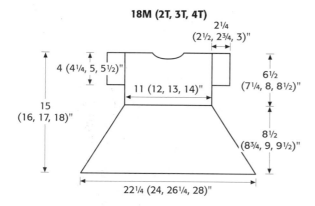

Materials

- Cascade Yarn's Madil Cotton Cable, 50-gram skeins (123 yds), 100% combed cotton
  Color A   4 (5, 5, 6) skeins #002 Black
  Color B   1 (1, 1, 1) skein #562 Red
  Color C   1 (1, 1, 1) skein #580 Ecru
- Size 6 needles: circular (24" and 16") or straight
- 2 decorative buttons (optional) (buttons shown are Mill Hill)
- Size G crochet hook
- Stitch holders

Gauge

22 sts and 28 rows = 4" in pattern stitch
To save time, always check your gauge. If necessary, change needle size to obtain correct gauge.

Pattern Stitch

Baby Cable Rib (multiple of 4 stitches plus 2)

Rows 1 and 3 (WS): K2, *P2, K2; repeat from *.

Row 2: P2, *K2, P2; repeat from *.

Row 4: P2, *K2tog, but leave on needle; then insert right needle between the 2 sts just knitted tog, and knit the first st again; then sl both sts from needle tog; P2; repeat from *.

Repeat Rows 1–4.

Skirt

In Color A, CO 244 (264, 288, 308) sts.

Round 1: Purl.

Rounds 2–4: Knit.

Rounds 5–16: Work Bottom Border Design, following the graph on page 111. After you complete the graphed design, cont knitting rounds until skirt measures 8½ (8¾, 9, 9½)".

Next round: K2tog around until 122 (132, 144, 154) sts rem. Divide sts into 2 equal sections for front and back bodice. Place back sts on a st holder. Now work back and forth as if using straight needles.

Bodice Front

Row 1 (RS): Knit across row, increasing 1 (0, 2, 1) sts in row to adjust number of sts for baby cable rib patt.

Row 2 (WS): Beg working baby cable rib patt and cont until garment measures 13 (13½, 14, 14½)". Beg front neck shaping.

Front Neck Shaping

WHEN GARMENT measures 13 (13½, 14, 14½)", work 20 (22, 24, 26) sts in patt; place next 22 (22, 26, 26) sts on holder; attach a second ball of yarn and work remaining 20 (22, 24, 26) sts. Dec 1 st at neck edge every row 4x. Cont in patt until garment measures 15 (16, 17, 18)". BO shoulder sts or place on st holder for seam method of preference.

Back Bodice

WORK SAME as bodice front, omitting front neck shaping. Cont in patt until garment measures 15 (16, 17, 18)". On next row, BO off first 16 (18, 20, 22) sts for right shoulder. Work across rem 30 (30, 34, 34) sts and place them on a holder. Then place the rem 16 (18, 20, 22) sts on a holder. Work in the reverse for the left shoulder. BO shoulder sts or place on st holder for seam method of preference. Join shoulder seams.

Sleeves

THE SLEEVES are knitted from the top down. They are not knitted in the round, but you can use circular needles if you wish. Measure 4 (4½, 5, 5½)" from shoulder seams in both directions and insert a st marker. With RS facing, PU 44 (50, 55, 60) sts evenly between markers. Work in St st until

sleeve measures 1¼ (1½, 1¾, 2)". On next row, dec 10 (10, 12, 12) sts evenly across row. Switch to Color B and work Row 12 (top row) of Bottom Border Design as shown on graph. In Color A, work 4 rows in St st. On next row, in Color C, cont in St st across row. BO sts in Color C.

Rolled Neck Edge

WITH RS facing, beg at back opening in Color A, PU 72 (80, 90, 98) sts. Work 8 rows in St st. BO sts loosely.

Finishing

SEW SLEEVE and side seams. In Color B, single crochet around skirt hem. Optional: place 2 decorative buttons on left front (see photo) and secure with contrasting yarn or ribbon.

Bottom Border Design

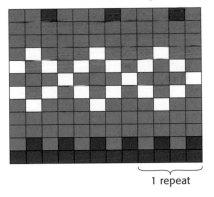

1 repeat

Design is 4 stitches x 12 rows.

Color Key

■ Color A: Black
■ Color B: Red
□ Color C: Ecru

Let It Snow

Holiday pictures are brought to life with this cheerful cardigan. Designed to coordinate with "Winter Wonderland," this festive cardigan can be worn over any black or red outfit to a holiday ice-skating party.

Let It Snow

This pattern is sized 2T (4T, 6).

●

FINISHED MEASUREMENTS

Chest: 26 (28, 30)"

Length: 12 (14, 16)"

Sleeve: 10 (11, 13)"

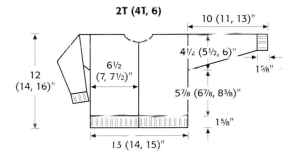

2T (4T, 6)

Materials

- Cascade Yarn's Madil Cotton Cable, 50-gram skeins (123 yds), 100% cotton
  Color A   3 (4, 5) skeins #562 Red
  Color B   2 (2, 2) skeins #002 Black
  Color C   1 (1, 1) skein #580 Ecru
- Size 5 needles: circular (16") or straight
- Size 6 needles: circular (24") or straight
- 6 (7, 7) buttons (buttons shown are bobbles, as explained in "Finishing" on page 115)
- Bobbins

- Stitch holders
- Stitch markers

Gauge

24 stitches and 30 rows = 4" in pattern stitch
To save time, always check your gauge. If necessary, change needle size to obtain correct gauge.

Pattern Stitch

Baby Cable Rib (multiple of 4 stitches plus 2)

Rows 1 and 3 (WS): K2; *P2, K2; repeat from *.

Row 2 (RS): P2; *K2, P2; repeat from *.

Row 4: P2; *K2tog, but leave on needle, insert right-hand needle between the 2 sts just knitted tog and knit the first again, then sl both sts from needle tog; P2; repeat from *.

Back

THIS SWEATER is not knitted in the round, but you can use circular needles if you wish. On size 6 needles, in Color B, CO 78 (86, 94) sts.

Rows 1–12: Work baby cable rib for 3 repeats. Beg Row 1 with Color B; complete ribbing in Color A. Row 13: Purl row, dec 0 (2, 0) sts and inc 0 (0, 2) sts to adjust sts for design graphs. Rows 14–35: Work Graph #1 for 22 rows. At the completion of design, in Color A, St st on 2 (4, 6) rows. Refer to Graph #2 and place as instructed on next 13 rows. In Color A, work St st patt on back sts (see Graph #3). When back measures 11½ (13½, 15½)", beg back neck shaping.

Back Neck Shaping

ON RS row, work patt on 25 (27, 31) sts; place 28 (30, 34) sts on holder; attach yarn and cont on 25 (27, 31) sts. Cont in est patt, dec 1 st at each neck edge every row 2x. When back measures 12 (14, 16)", BO shoulder sts or place on st holder for seam method of preference.

Left Front

IN COLOR B, CO 38 (46, 50) sts. Work Rows 1–12 as for back. Row 13: To adjust sts for design work, dec 2 (4, 2) sts in row. Rows 14–35: Same as back. Cont as for back through completion of the 14-row Let It Snow Design (Graph #2). Now work 3 rows of St st in Color A. In last row of St st, inc 2 (4, 2) sts evenly. Work baby cable rib for 4 (6, 7) repeats as follows: In Color A, 2 (4, 5) cables plus 2 rows of cable 3 (5, 6); in Color C, 2 rows that complete cable 3 (5, 6) and 1 row of cable 4 (6,7); in Color B, 3 rem rows of cable 4 (6, 7). Cont St st in Color B; see Graph #3 for placing 1 st of Color C in row. When front measures 10 (11½, 13½)", beg left front neck and shoulder shaping.

Left Front Neck and Shoulder Shaping

AT NECK edge, BO 8 (11, 13) sts, cont on rem 28 (31, 35) sts in patt. For shoulder shaping, dec 1 st at neck edge EOR 5 (6, 6)x. Work in patt until garment measures 12 (14, 16)". BO shoulder sts or leave on st holder for seam method of preference.

Right Front

WORK SAME as for left front. Beg right front neck and shoulder shaping.

Right Front Neck and Shoulder Shaping

REVERSE SHAPING as for left front and work in patt until garment measures 12 (14, 16)". BO shoulder sts or place on st holder for seam method of preference. Join shoulder seams.

Sleeves

THE SLEEVES are knitted from the top down. They are not knitted in the round, but you can use circular needles if you wish. Beg 4½ (5½, 6)" from shoulder seam, mark back and front distance from shoulder before picking up sleeve sts. With RS facing, beg at one marker in Color B, PU 58 (66, 74) sts, dividing sts evenly between front and back markers. Baby cable rib rows and Rows 1–15 of Let It Snow Bottom Border (Graph #1) are worked in reverse order in working the sleeve from the top down. Work in St st with Graph #1 in Color B and Color C until sleeve measures 2 (2½, 3½)", ending with WS row. Next row, beg baby cable rib as follows: Row 4, 3, 2 in Color B; Row 1, 4, 3 in Color C; Row 2 and all rem rows in Color A. At 5½ (6, 7)", staying in patt, dec 1 st at each end of row every sixth row 2 (3, 4)x. Cont in patt until sleeve measures 7 (8, 10)". Beg with Row 13 and work Let It Snow Bottom Border patt on 54 (60, 66) sts from Row 13 down to Row 2. In Row 1, dec 16 (18, 20) sts evenly across row. On size 5 needles, in baby cable rib, work 3 patt repeats for cuff as follows: Color A, 10 rows; Color B, 1 row. BO loosely in Color B.

Button Band

WITH RS of work facing and size 5 needles, in Color C, PU 58 (66, 78) sts along left front edge. Work in K2, P2 rib for 7 rows. BO in Color B. Repeat for right front, placing 6 (7, 7) buttonholes (K2tog, yo) in fourth row evenly on band. Place first buttonhole 2 sts down from top. For more information on buttonholes, see pages 16–18.

Neck Ribbing

WITH RS facing and size 5 needles, in Color C, PU 86 (90, 98) sts around neck, including back sts on holder and top of button band.

Row 1 (WS): P2, K2 across row.

Row 2 (RS): K2, P2 across row.

Rows 3–4: Repeat Rows 1–2.

Rows 5-6: On size 6 needle, repeat Rows 1-2.

Rows 7–15: Work in St st.

Row 16: In Color B, BO loosely.

Finishing

JOIN SLEEVE and side seams. Sew on buttons to correspond with buttonholes. Model garment buttons are bobbles made in Color A.

Bobble

IN APPROPRIATE yarn color, leaving a 5" tail of yarn, CO 5 sts. K1, P1, K1, P1, K1; turn and repeat for 4 rows. BO in K1, P1 pattern. Leave 5" tail of yarn. Tie the yarn tails together tightly, forming a ball. Pull yarn tails through to wrong side of garment. Tie off yarn tails and clip ends of yarn.

Graph#1: Let It Snow Bottom Border

Color Key
- ■ Color A: Red
- ▨ Color B: Black
- □ Color C: Ecru

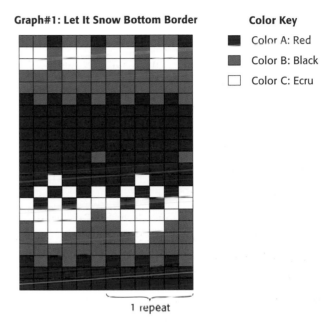

1 repeat

Design is worked in St st and repeated as needed for number of sts on back and front.

Graph #2: Let It Snow Snowflake

Design repeat is 26 stitches.

Back

2T (78 sts): Beg on Row 8; place 3 snowflakes; end Row 33.

4T (84 sts): Beg on Row 5; place 3 snowflakes; end Row 34.

6 (96 sts): Beg on Row 12; place 4 snowflakes; end Row 3.

Front

2T (36 sts): Beg on Row 3; place 1 snowflake; end Row 38.

4T (42 sts): Beg on Row 13; place 2 snowflakes; end Row 2.

6 (48 sts): Beg on Row 10; place 2 snowflakes; end Row 5.

Graph #3: Let It Snow Stockinette Stitch Pattern

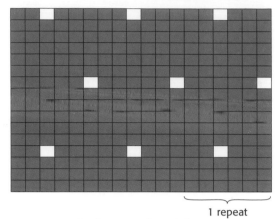

1 repeat

Design repeat is 6 stitches.

Repeat Rows 1–16 as needed per instructions. All open spaces are worked in color stated in pattern.

This trendy tunic will look great on your grand-daughter or grandson. Scottie dogs are classic; they are always in style. This design came from a coloring book.

Sassy Scotties

This pattern is sized 18M (2T, 3T, 4T).

●

FINISHED MEASUREMENTS

Chest: 24 (26, 27, 28)"

Length: 13 (14, 15, 16)"

Drop Sleeve: 8 (9, 10, 11)"

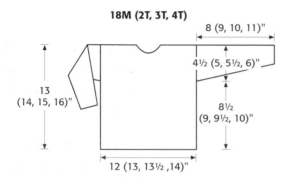

18M (2T, 3T, 4T)

8 (9, 10, 11)"

4½ (5, 5½, 6)"

13 (14, 15, 16)"

8½ (9, 9½, 10)"

12 (13, 13½ ,14)"

Materials

- Tahki Cotton Classic, 50-gram skeins (108 yds), 100% cotton
  Color A   3 (3, 3, 4) skeins #3997 Red
  Color B   1 (1, 1, 2) skeins #3002 Black
  Color C   1 (1, 1, 1) skein #3001 White
- Size 6 needles: circular (24" and 16"). If desired, straight needles can be used for the sleeves.
- Stitch holders
- Stitch markers
- Size F crochet hook

Gauge

22 stitches and 28 rows = 4" in pattern stitches
To save time, always check your gauge. If necessary, change needle size to obtain correct gauge.

Pattern Stitch

SEE SCOTTIE Design graph on page 119.

Back and Front

THIS GARMENT is knitted in the round. In Color A, CO 132 (142, 148, 154) sts.

Round 1: Purl.

Round 2: Knit.

Round 3: Purl.

Round 4: Work in St st as follows: 3 rounds in Color A; 6 rounds of checkerboard as follows: *K2 in Color B; K2 in Color A; repeat from * for 2 rounds. Reverse Colors A and B for 2 rounds. Reverse again for the last 2 rounds. Knit 3 rounds in Color A; purl next round in Color A. Cont in St st as follows: 2 rounds in Color A; 1 round in Color C; 1 round in Color A; 2 rounds in Color B; 3 (4, 5, 6) rounds in Color A; 3 rounds in Color B; 4 (5, 6, 7) rounds in Color C; 2 rounds in Color A; 6 (7, 8, 9) rounds in Color B; 4 (5, 6, 7) rounds in Color A. At this point, divide sts into 2 sections for front and back.

Front

DISCONTINUE WORKING in the round and beg to work back and forth as if using straight needles. In Color C, cont in St st for 3 (4, 5, 6) rows. Beg working Scottie Design, referring to the graph on page 119. Place 3 Scottie dogs evenly across front (and back) of garment for a total of 6. After Scottie

Design is completed, cont in St st in Color C for 3 (4, 5, 6) rows. Change to Color A and work 14 (15, 15, 15) rows. Beg front neck shaping.

Front Neck Shaping

ON NEXT row, work 22 (23, 24, 24) sts; place next 22 (25, 26, 29) sts on st holder; attach second ball of yarn and work rem 22 (23, 24, 24) sts. Working shoulders at same time, cont in St st, dec 1 st every row at each neck edge 4x. Work rem 18 (19, 20, 20) sts until front measures 13 (14, 15, 16)". BO shoulder sts or place on st holder for seam method of preference.

Back

REPEAT FRONT instructions, omitting front neck shaping. Cont working in Color A until piece measures 13 (14, 15, 16)". Beg back neck shaping.

Back Neck Shaping

WITH RS facing, BO the 18 (19, 20, 20) shoulder sts or place them on a st holder. Place center 30 (33, 34, 37) sts on a holder. Join shoulder seams.

Sleeves

THE SLEEVES are knitted from the top down. They are not knitted in the round, but you can use circular needles if you wish. Measure 4½ (5, 5½, 6)" from shoulder seam; mark back and front distance from shoulder before picking up sleeve sts.

With RS facing, beg at 1 marker, PU 50 (55, 60, 66) sts evenly between front and back markers. Work in Color A in St st until sleeve measures 5½ (6½, 7½, 8½)", ending with WS row. Purl next row. Repeat the checkerboard patt, dec 1 st at each edge EOR. Work next 3 rows in St st, continuing to dec 1 st at each edge EOR. On next row, in garter st (knit every row), dec 4 (7, 8, 10) sts evenly across row. On rem sts, work 2 rows of garter st. BO for cuff.

Neck Edge

WITH RS of garment facing, in Color A, PU 80 (86, 90, 96) sts for neck edging. Knit 3 rounds in garter st. BO edging.

Finishing

SEW SIDE and sleeve seams tog. In Color B, single crochet around tunic bottom, sleeve cuff, and neck edge. Red ribbon bows can be tied around the necks of the dogs. Knot securely.

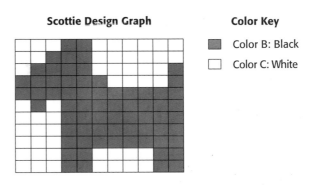

Scottie Design Graph

Color Key
■ Color B: Black
□ Color C: White

Each Scottie is 11 stitches x 11 rows.

Wave Runner

Every toddler's wardrobe needs a one-piece romper.
This is a fast project and so comfortable for little girls
to wear. Leave the ruffle off the collar, and you'll
have a cute garment that any little boy will love.

Wave Runner

This pattern is sized 18M (2T, 3T).

●

FINISHED MEASUREMENTS

Chest: 24 (26, 29)"

Length: 18 (19, 20)"

Sleeve: 1½ (2½, 3)"

18M (2T, 3T)

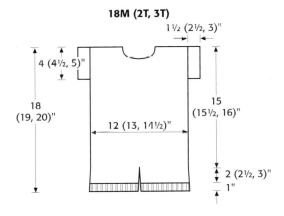

Materials

- Tahki Cotton Classic, 50-gram skeins (108 yds), 100% cotton

Color A 3912	3 (3, 4) skeins #3912 Purple
Color B 3726	2 (2, 2) skeins #3726 Green
Color C 3001	1 (1, 1) skein #3001 White

- Size 6 needles: circular (24"). If desired, straight needles can be used for the sleeves.
- Stitch holders
- 5 buttons (buttons shown are JHB)

Gauge

22 stitches and 28 rows = 4" in pattern stitches

To save time, always check your gauge. If necessary, change needle size to obtain correct gauge.

Pattern Stitches

Stripe Pattern

Rows 1–5: St st in Color A.

Row 6: K1, P1 across in Color B.

Rows 7–10: St st in Color B.

Rows 11–13: St st in Color A.

Rows 14–15: St st in Color C.

Repeat Rows 1–15.

Seed Stitch

Row 1 (RS): K1, P1 across row.

Row 2 (WS): Purl the knit sts and knit the purl sts.

Repeat Rows 1 and 2.

Pants

In Color B, CO 56 (60, 66) sts for each leg (working both legs at the same time). Work back and forth on the circular needles. Rows 1–6: K2, P2. In Color A, beg working in stripe patt, inc 1 st at each edge every third row 5 (6, 7)x. When pants measure 3 (3½, 4)", beg crotch shaping.

Crotch Shaping

On next row with RS facing, join legs. Now you will be working in the round with 132 (144, 160) sts on the needles. Cont until garment measures 9 (9½, 10)". Create placket opening.

Placket Opening

DIVIDE STS in the middle of the front, and start working back and forth on the needle. Cont working in est stripe patt. When garment measures 14 (14½, 15)", beg armhole shaping.

Armhole Shaping

DIVIDE STS into 3 sections for front and back. Each front section has 33 (36, 40) sts; back section has 66 (72, 80) sts. Place back sts on st holder. Working both of the front sections at the same time, cont in stripe patt until front measures 16½ (17½, 18½)". Beg neck shaping.

Neck Shaping

BO 6 (7, 8) sts at each neck edge. Cont working in patt, dec 1 st at each neck edge every row 5x. When garment measures 18 (19, 20)", BO shoulder sts or place on st holder for seam method of preference.

Back

PICKING UP the sts from holder, work back same as front, omitting the neck shaping until garment measures 18 (19, 20)". BO the 19 (20, 22) sts or place them on a st holder for seam method of preference. Place 28 (32, 36) sts on st holder. Join shoulder seams.

Sleeves

THE SLEEVES are knitted from the top down. They are not knitted in the round, but you can use circular needles if you wish. With RS facing in Color A, PU 44 (50, 55) sts along armhole opening. Work in St st until sleeve measures 1½ (2, 2½)". On next row, dec 10 (12, 14) sts evenly across row. In Color B, K1, P1 across. On next row, knit across. On final row, knit across. BO sts for cuff.

Front Placket

WITH RS facing in Color B, PU 40 (44, 48) sts along left front opening. Work 4 rows of K1, P1 seed st. BO. Pick up the same number of sts along front opening for right placket. Work 4 rows of seed st, placing 5 buttonholes (K2tog, yo), evenly spaced, down placket. For more information on buttonholes, see pages 16–18. BO.

Collar

WITH WS facing in Color C, PU 56 (62, 68) sts around neck edge, including the back sts on st holder. Working back and forth on the needles, work 8 rows of K1, P1 Seed st. To create collar ruffle, inc 2 sts in each st on next row. Work next 4 rows in K4, P4 across. BO in K4, P4.

Finishing

SEW CROTCH seam tog. Sew sleeve seams tog. Sew buttons onto left front placket in Color A. Tack collar down in front.

Cascade Yarn's denim yarn in ecru and taupe inspired this two-piece outfit. Adding sailboat buttons gave an otherwise simple design a bit of distinction. Roomy pants that tie at the waist make for an easy on-and-off, even for a tyke in diapers.

Nautical Number

This pattern is sized 18M (2T, 3T, 4T).

●

FINISHED MEASUREMENTS

Chest: 24 (26, 27, 28)"

Top Length: 11 (12, 13, 14)"

Sleeve: 4½ (5½, 6½, 7½)"

Pant Length: 10¼ (10¾, 11¼, 11¾)"

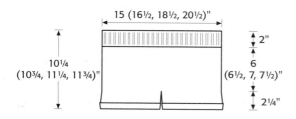

Materials

- Cascade Yarn's Madil Denim, 50-gram skeins (137 yds), 60% cotton/40% acrylic
  Color A 047   2 (2, 2, 3) skeins Ecru
  Color B 048   3 (3, 3, 4) skeins Taupe
- Size 6 needles: circular (24"). If desired, straight needles can be used for the sleeves.
- Size G crochet hook
- Stitch holders
- Large-eyed sewing needle
- 2 buttons (model buttons are Trendsetter)

Gauge

22 stitches and 28 rows = 4" in pattern stitches
To save time, always check your gauge. If necessary, change needle size to obtain correct gauge.

Pattern Stitches

Stripe Pattern

Rows 1–4: St st in Color B.

Row 5: K1, P1 across in Color A.

Rows 6–10: St st in Color A.

Repeat this 10-row patt.

Seed Stitch

Row 1 (RS): K1, P1 across row.

Row 2 (WS): Purl the knit sts and knit the purl sts.
Repeat Rows 1 and 2.

Top

To create a side vent, in Color A, CO 2 sections of 66 (72, 76, 78) sts each. Working each section back and forth on the needle, work in seed st for 5 rows. On next row, beg stripe patt, leaving 5 sts at each end of each section to be worked in seed st. Continue in stripe patt until you have completed 8 stripes. At this point, join work and beg knitting in the round. Cont in stripe patt until top measures 7 (7½, 8, 8½)". Divide sts on needle back into the 2 sections for front and back. Place back sts on st holder. With front sts on the needle, work back and forth in stripe patt until front measures 9½ (10½, 11½, 12)". Beg boat neck shaping.

Boat Neck Shaping

With RS facing, work across 15 (17, 18, 18) sts. Place the center 36 (38, 40, 42) sts on st holder. Join second ball of yarn and work rem 15 (17, 18, 18) sts. Working in stripe patt, dec 1 st at each neck edge every row 4x. Cont in patt until garment measures 11 (12, 13, 14)". Place shoulder sts on st holders.

Back

Work back same as front until back measures 11 (12, 13, 14)". Beg boat neck edging.

Boat Neck Edging

In Color A, work first shoulder sts in seed st; PU 6 sts along first neck edge; PU center sts on holder; PU 6 sts along second neck edge; and work second shoulder sts in seed st. Work in seed st for 6 rows. BO neck edge. Repeat with front shoulders and neck edge. In Color A, single crochet along front and back shoulder and neck edges. Lay back shoulders over front shoulders and tack down along shoulder. Sew a button on front at each shoulder.

Sleeves

The sleeves are knitted from the top down. They are not knitted in the round, but you can use circular needles if you wish. In Color A with RS facing, PU 44 (50, 55, 60) sts evenly around armhole opening. Work in stripe patt, dec 1 st at each edge every inch until sleeve measures 4 (5, 6, 7)". In Color B, work 5 final rows of seed st. BO cuff.

Pants

The pants are worked from the top down on circular needles. In Color B, CO 110 (120, 136, 150) sts. Work in K1, P1 ribbing for 12 rounds. On next round, inc 1 st in every other st until there are 165 (180, 204, 225) sts on the needles. Cont knitting rounds until garment measures 7½ (8, 8½, 9)". Beg crotch shaping: Divide sts into 2 equal sections. Knitting back and forth on the needles, dec 1 st at each edge EOR. Cont until pants measure 9½ (10, 10½, 11)". Beg cuff: On next row, K2tog every other st across row. Work 5 rows of seed st for each cuff. BO.

Finishing

Sew sleeve seams tog. Sew crotch seams tog. Single crochet a chain of Color B and weave through waistband. Create a tassel at each end of waistband tie. For more information on tassels, see page 27.

Fruit Loops

This sassy skimmer celebrates the ribbon craze. Satin ribbon on big needles makes this project fun and fast.

Fruit Loops

This pattern is sized 2T (4T, 6).

●

FINISHED MEASUREMENTS

Chest: 27 (29, 31)"

Length: 8 1/2 (10, 12)"

Sleeve: 3"

2T (4T, 6)

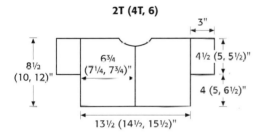

Materials

- Satin (made exclusively in Italy for Tahki Imports, Ltd.), 50-gram skeins (98 yds), 87% cotton/13% nylon
  Color A   2 (2, 2) skeins #9001 White
  Color B   1 (1, 1) skein #9005 Aqua
  Color C   1 (1, 1) skein #9003 Orange
  Color D   1 (1, 1) skein #9007 Yellow
- Size 10 1/2 needles: circular (24") or straight
- 3 (4, 4) buttons (model buttons are JHB International)
- Stitch holders

Gauge

16 stitches and 22 rows = 4" in pattern stitches
To save time, always check your gauge. If necessary, change needle size to obtain correct gauge.

Pattern Stitches

Loop Stitch

See explanation in pattern instructions.

Garter Stitch

Knit every row.

Back

THIS SWEATER is not knitted in the round, but you can use circular needles to work back and forth, treating both front sections as one piece to armhole opening. In Color B, CO 108 (116, 124) sts. Beg working loop stitch as follows:

Rows 1–4: Knit.

Row 5 (WS): K1, *Hold the middle finger of your left hand behind the needles as shown so that this finger gets caught by the yarn as you bring it around, and K1 more st; however, do not slip this knitted st off the needle at this time. Transfer the loop you just pulled through this st back onto the left needle. Then K the 2 loops on the left needle tog through the back of the loops. Then remove your finger from the loop and remove the sts to the right needle. Repeat from * in every st across row.

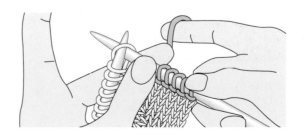

Row 6 (RS): Knit through back loop of every st across row.

In Color C, repeat Rows 1–6 above.

In Color D, work as follows:

Row 1 (WS): Knit.

Row 2 (RS): K1, *yo, K2tog; repeat from *, ending K1.

Row 3: Purl.

Row 4: Knit.

In Color A, work in St st for 1". On next row, divide sts into 1 back and 2 front sections by working 27 (29, 31) sts and placing them on a st holder for 1 shoulder; cont in St st on 54 (58, 62) sts; place rem 27 (29, 31) sts on st holder for second shoulder. Cont in St st on back sts only; work until garment measures 8¼ (9¾, 11¾)" from beg. On next row, work across 17 (18, 19) sts; BO 20 (22, 24) sts; work rem 17 (18, 19) sts. Cont on each shoulder, if necessary, until back section measures 8½ (10, 12)". BO shoulder sts or place on st holder for seam method of preference.

Left Front

PICK UP 27 (29, 31) sts from st holder and work in St st until front section measures 8 (9½, 11½)" from beg. On next RS row, work across 17 (18, 19) sts and BO rem 10 (11, 12) sts. Attach yarn and continue on shoulder sts until front measures 8½ (10, 12)". BO shoulder sts or place on st holder for seam method of preference.

Right Front

WORK SAME as left front except reverse shaping for neck. At neck edge on RS row, BO 10 (11, 12) sts and cont on rem 17 (18, 19) sts. Work shoulder as for left front. Join shoulder seams.

Sleeves

THE SLEEVES are knitted from the top down. They are not knitted in the round, but you can use circular needles if you wish. Measure 4½ (5, 5½)" from shoulder seams in both directions and insert a st marker. With RS facing in Color D, PU 36 (40, 44) sts evenly between markers. Work as follows:

Row 1 (WS): Knit.

Row 2 (RS): Purl.

Rows 3–4: Repeat Rows 1–2.

Row 5: Knit.

Row 6: K1, *yo, K2tog; repeat from *, ending K1.

Row 7: Purl.

Row 8: Knit. In Color C, repeat Rows 5–8. In Color B, repeat Rows 5–8.

Next row (WS): Knit. BO loosely in Color B.

Front Ribbing

ON RIGHT front edge, in Color A, PU 36 (42, 52) sts evenly along edge. Work in garter st for 7 rows. BO loosely. Repeat for left front ribbing, placing 3 (4, 4) buttonholes (K2tog, yo), evenly spaced, in fourth row of garter st. Buttonhole should accommodate a ¾"-diameter button. For more information on buttonholes, see pages 16–18.

Neck Edging

ON RS of garment, beg at front edge of ribbing in Color A, PU 56 (60, 64) sts evenly around neck edge. On next row, knit. BO loosely around neck.

Finishing

SEW SLEEVE and side seams tog. Sew on buttons to correspond with buttonholes.

Styled like an aviator's jacket, this design works up beautifully in bulky Cascade Pastaza yarn. Hunter green and camel are the perfect colors for this great jacket. (Our model wanted to take this one home!)

Tally Ho!

This pattern is sized 2T (4T, 6).

•

FINISHED MEASUREMENTS

Chest: 28 (32, 35)"

Length: 13 (15, 17)"

Sleeve: 10 (11, 12)"

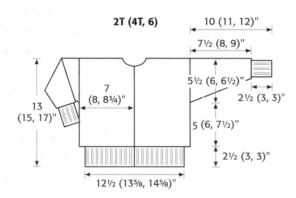

Materials

- Cascade Pastaza, 100-gram skeins (132 yds), 50% llama/50% wool

  Color A   4 (5, 6) skeins #052 Green

  Color B   1 (1, 1) skein #009 Camel
- Size 8 needles: circular (24") or straight
- Size 10 1/2 needles: circular (24") or straight
- Cable needle
- 12 (14, 16)" separating zipper
- Stitch holders
- Stitch markers
- Large-eyed sewing needle
- Cotton sewing thread

Gauge

20 stitches and 24 rows = 4" in rib st

22 stitches and 26 rows = 4" in baby cable rib

To save time, always check your gauge. If necessary, change needle size to obtain correct gauge.

Pattern Stitches

Baby Cable Rib (multiple of 4 stitches plus 2)

Rows 1 and 3 (WS): K2, *P2, K2; repeat from *.

Row 2 (RS): P2, *K2, P2; repeat from *.

Row 4: P2, *K2tog, but leave on needle; then insert right needle between the 2 sts just knitted tog, and knit the first again; then sl both sts from needle tog, P2; repeat from *.

Repeat Rows 1–4.

Cable Pattern (multiple of 12 stitches)

Row 1 (WS): Purl all sts on all WS rows.

Row 2 (RS): K2, P2, *sl next 3 sts to cable needle and hold in back, K3, then K3 from cn; sl next 3 sts to cn and hold in front; K3, then K3 from cn; repeat from *; end P2, K2.

Rows 4, 6, and 8: Knit.

Repeat Rows 1–8.

Seed Stitch

Row 1 (RS): K1, P1 across row.

Row 2 (WS): Purl the knit sts and knit the purl sts.

Repeat Rows 1 and 2.

Front and Back

THIS GARMENT is not worked in the round, but you can use circular needles if you wish. On size 8 needles, in Color A, CO 126 (134, 146) sts. Working back and forth on needles in baby cable rib, work 2 rows in Color B and rem rows in Color A for 3 (4, 4) repeats of patt. On next row, inc 26 (30, 42) sts evenly across for a total of 152 (164, 188) sts for body of garment. Change to larger needles and in Color B, work 1 row in St st. Beg cable patt in Color A, and work until garment measures 6½ (8, 9½)". On next row, divide sts into 3 sections, creating 2 front sections and a back section: In patt, work 37 (40, 46) sts; cont on 78 (84, 96) sts and place on st holder for back section; work patt on rem 37 (40, 46) sts. At the side opening where patt cannot be completed, work as much of the patt as possible and knit rem sts. Cont patt on each front section until each measures 12 (14, 16)". Beg front neck shaping.

Front Neck Shaping

AT EACH front neck edge, BO 14 (16, 18) sts. Cont to work in est pattern, dec 1 st at neck edge every row 2x. BO rem 21 (22, 26) shoulder sts or place them on a st holder for seam method of preference.

Back Neck Shaping

PU STS from st holder and continue in cable patt until back measures 13 (15, 17)". BO the 21 (22, 26) shoulder sts or place them on a st holder for seam method of preference. Place the center 36 (40, 44) sts on st holder until the collar is knit. BO 21 (22, 26) sts for second shoulder.

Shoulder Epaulets

MAKE 2.

With size 10½ needles, in Color A, CO 10 sts. Work in St st as follows: 1 st in Color A, 2 sts in Color B, 4 sts in Color A, 2 sts in Color B, 1 st in Color A. Work as est until epaulet measures 4¾ (5, 5½)". BO. Place epaulet lengthwise between front and back shoulder edges and sew each edge in place.

Sleeves

THE SLEEVES are knitted from the top down. They are not knitted in the round, but you can use circular needles if you wish. Measure 5½ (6, 6½)" from center edge of epaulet and insert a st marker. With RS facing and using the larger needles, in Color A, PU 42 (46, 50) sts evenly between markers. Work in seed st until sleeve measures 7½ (9½, 10½)", ending on RS row. On next row, change to size 8 needles, dec 8 sts evenly across row. Beg working cuff on rem 34 (38, 42) sts. Cuff is worked in 3 repeats of baby cable rib. Work Rows 1–2 in Color B. Work Rows 3–4 in Color A. Cont in Color A until you finish 3 repeats of patt. Change to Color B and work Rows 1–2. BO loosely in Color A.

Collar

WITH RS of garment facing and with size 8 needles, in Color A, pick up 94 (98, 106) sts, including sts on back st holder. Collar is worked in baby cable rib as follows: 1 repeat in Color A; 4 (4, 5) repeats in Color B. BO loosely in Color A.

Finishing

WITH RS of work facing, place zipper so that the teeth show in front openings. Pin zipper securely in place. Turn garment to wrong side and hand sew zipper, using regular cotton sewing thread. At collar edge, tuck and secure zipper tabs under, toward the wrong side of garment, to give a more finished look. Sew sleeves and remaining side openings tog. Block very carefully; do not put heat too close to this garment or it will flatten the cables.

Chow Chow

Hooded and warm—this red, white, and blue jacket works for all seasons. Knit it in Tahki's Cotton Classic II yarn, which is a heavier weight/gauge yarn—perfect for chilly fall days.

Chow Chow

This pattern is sized 18M (2T, 4T).

●

FINISHED MEASUREMENTS

Chest: 23 (26, 29)"

Length: 11 (13, 15)"

Sleeve: 9 (10, 12)"

18M (2T, 4T)

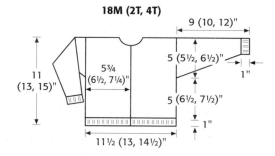

Materials

- Tahki Cotton Classic II, 50-gram skeins (74 yds), 100% cotton
  Color A   3 (4, 4) skeins #2874 Blue
  Color B   2 (3, 3) skeins #2997 Red
  Color C   2 (3, 3) skeins #2003 Ecru
- Size 8 needles: circular (24") or straight
- 5 (5, 6) buttons (buttons shown are JHB International)
- Stitch holders

Gauge

22 stitches and 24 rows = 4" in pattern stitch

18 stitches and 24 rows = 4" in St st for sleeves and hood

To save time, always check your gauge. If necessary, change needle size to obtain correct gauge.

Back

THIS GARMENT is not knitted in the round, but you can use circular needles if you wish. In Color A, CO 64 (72, 80) sts. Work in P2, K2 ribbing for 7 rows.

Next row (RS): Beg back color pattern as follows:

Row 1: *K4 sts in Color B, K4 sts in Color C; repeat from * to end of row.

Row 2: Purl sts in est color.

Rows 3–4: Repeat Rows 1–2.

Row 5: In Color B, knit across.

Row 6: In Color B, purl across.

Row 7: *K4 sts in Color C, K4 sts in Color B; repeat from * to end of row.

Row 8: Purl sts in est color.

Rows 9–10: Repeat Rows 7–8.

Row 11: In Color B, knit across.

Row 12: In Color B, purl across.

Repeat Rows 1–12 for garment back.

Cont working back section in est color patt until back measures 10 (12, 14)" from beg. Beg back neck and shoulder shaping.

Back Neck and Shoulder Shaping

SHOULDERS CAN be worked separately or at the same time by attaching a second ball of yarn. Next RS row, work 20 (23, 26) sts; BO 24 (26, 28) sts; work 20 (23, 26) sts for second shoulder. Cont in patt on shoulder sts, dec 1 st at neck edge EOR 2x until 18 (21, 24) sts rem. When garment measures 11 (13, 15)" from beg, BO shoulder sts or place on st holder for seam method of preference.

Left Front

IN COLOR A, CO 32 (36, 40) sts. Work in P2, K2 ribbing for 7 rows. On next row (RS), beg left front color pattern as follows:

Row 1 (sizes 18M, 4T): * K4 sts in Color A, K4 sts in Color C; repeat from * to end of row.

Row 1 (size 2T): *K4 sts in Color C, K4 sts in Color A; repeat from * to end of row.

Row 2: Purl sts in est color.

Rows 3–4: Repeat Rows 1–2.

Row 5: In Color A, knit across.

Row 6: In Color A, purl across.

Row 7 (sizes 18M, 4T): *K4 sts in Color C, K4 sts in Color A; repeat from * to end of row.

Row 7 (size 2T): *K4 sts in Color A, K4 sts in Color C; repeat from * to end of row.

Row 8: Purl sts in est color.

Rows 9–10: Repeat Rows 7–8.

Row 11: In Color A, knit across.

Row 12: In Color A, purl across.

Repeat Rows 1–12 for left front. Work left front in color patt until garment measures 9½ (10½, 12½)" from beg. On next WS row at front neck edge, BO 10 (11, 12) sts. Cont in color pattern, dec 1 st at neck edge EOR 4x until 18 (21, 24) sts rem. Cont in est patt until left front measures 11 (13, 15)". BO shoulder sts or place on st holder for seam method of preference.

Right Front

IN COLOR A, CO 32 (36, 40) sts. Work in P2, K2 ribbing for 7 rows. On next row (RS), beg right front color pattern as follows:

Row 1 (sizes 18M, 4T): *K4 sts in Color B, K4 sts in Color C; repeat from* to end of row.

Row 1 (size 2T): *K4 sts in Color C, K4 sts in Color B; repeat from * to end of row.

Row 2: Purl sts in est color.

Rows 3–4: Repeat Rows 1–2.

Row 5: In Color C, knit across.

Row 6: In Color C, purl across.

Row 7 (sizes 18M, 4T): *K4 sts in Color C, K4 sts in Color B; repeat from * to end of row.

Row 7 (size 2T): *K4 sts in Color B, K4 sts in Color C; repeat from * to end of row.

Row 8: Purl sts in est color.

Rows 9–10: Repeat Rows 7–8.

Row 11: In Color C, knit across.

Row 12: In Color C, purl across.

Repeat Rows 1–12 for right front.

Work right front in color patt until garment measures 9½ (10½, 12½)" from beg. On next RS row at front neck edge, BO 10 (11, 12) sts. Cont to work in color patt, dec 1 st at neck edge EOR 4x until 18 (21, 24) sts rem. Cont in est patt until right front measures 11 (13, 15)". BO shoulder sts or place on st holder for seam method of preference. Join shoulder seams.

Sleeves

The sleeves are knitted from the top down. They are not knitted in the round, but you can use circular needles if you wish. Measure 5 (5½, 6½)" from shoulder seams in both directions and insert st marker. With RS facing, in Color A, PU 50 (55, 65) sts evenly between markers. Work in St st until sleeve measures 5 (6, 7½)" from beg. On next row, dec 1 st at each edge EOR 7 (7, 8)x. Cont working in St st until sleeve measures 7½ (8½, 10½)". Change to Color C and work 3 rows, dec 4 (5, 7) sts evenly across last row. Beg cuff in Color B on rem 32 (36, 42) sts: Work in K2, P2 ribbing for 6 rows. BO loosely.

Neck Ribbing

With RS of garment facing, in Color B, PU 66 (74, 82) sts around neck edge. Work in P2, K2 ribbing for 5 rows. BO loosely.

Front Button Band

Do not include neck ribbing edge when picking up sts for button band. With RS of work facing, in Color A for left side front and Color B for right side front, PU 46 (50, 58) sts at front edge. Work in P2, K2 ribbing for 6 rows. Place 5 (5, 6) buttonholes (K2tog, yo), evenly spaced, in third row of button band, beg 2 sts from neck edge. Buttonholes go on the right front for girls, and on the left front for boys. For more information on buttonholes, see pages 16–18.

Hood

Hood is knitted separately and attached to the garment at neck ribbing. In Color A, CO 82 (86, 90) sts. Work in P2, K2 ribbing for 5 rows; change to Color B and work 3 more rows. Remainder of hood is worked in Color C in St st. Cont in St st, dec 1 st at each edge every 4 (5, 6) rows 6x. Cont until hood measures 7 (7½, 8)" from beg, ending on WS row. BO 5 sts at beg of next 2 rows. BO 4 sts at beg of next 6 rows. BO 0 (1, 2) sts at beg of next 2 rows. BO rem 36 (38, 40) sts.

Finishing

Sew side and sleeve seams. Sew back seam of hood. Sew base of hood to top of neck ribbing. Do not include button band. Make tassel of Colors A, B, and C and attach securely to the point of the hood. For more information on tassels, see page 27. Sew on buttons to correspond with the buttonholes.

Aye, Aye, Captain!

Your little skipper will sail along in this easy pullover jacket. This zippered pullover design has become one of our trademarks. Great in cotton, wool, or acrylic, it is so versatile. Consider using a sew-on emblem on your next solid-colored garment for a decorative touch.

Aye, Aye, Captain!

This pattern is sized 18M (2T, 4T).

●

FINISHED MEASUREMENTS

Chest: 25 (28, 30)"

Length: 12½(14, 16)"

Sleeve: 9 (10, 11½)"

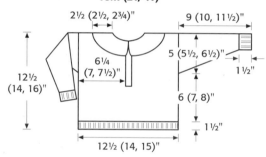

Materials

- Tahki Cotton Classic II, 50-gram skeins (74 yds), 100% cotton
  Color A   6 (7, 8) skeins Royal #2873
  Color B   2 (2, 2) skeins Red #2997
  Color C   A small amount of White #2001
- Size 8 needles: circular (24"). If desired, straight needles can also be used.
- 7" jumbo zipper
- Stitch holders
- Large-eyed sewing needle
- Cotton sewing thread
- Nautical appliqué patch (optional)

Gauge

18 stitches and 24 rows = 4" in pattern stitch
To save time, always check your gauge. If necessary, change needle size to obtain correct gauge.

Pattern Stitch

Basket Weave Stitch (knitted in the round)

Round 1: *K2, P2, repeat from * around.

Round 2: *K2, P2, repeat from * around to marker.

Round 3: *P2, K2, repeat from * around to marker.

Round 4: *P2, K2, repeat from * around.

Repeat this 4-round pattern.

Front and Back

THIS GARMENT is knitted partially in the round and partially back and forth. You may use circular needles for both. In Color B, CO 112 (124, 136) sts. Work in K1, P1 ribbing for 2 rounds. On next round, K1, P1 around in Color C. Switch back to Color B and work 7 (8, 9) rounds in K1, P1 ribbing. Switching to Color A, knit next round. Beg working in basket weave st as explained above. When work measures 5 (6, 6½)", divide sts into 3 sections, creating 1 back section and 2 front sections for zipper-placket opening. Back section has 56 (60, 68) sts; each front section has 28 (30, 34) sts. With yarn attached to each section, work each section in patt st, working back and forth as if using straight needles until front sections measure 11½ (12, 12½)". Place back section on a st holder. Beg front neck shaping.

Front Neck Shaping

AT EACH front neck edge, BO 8 (10, 10) sts. Cont to work in patt, dec 1 st every row at each neck edge, 6 (6, 6)x. Work rem 14 (15, 18) sts until each front piece measures 12½ (14, 16)". BO shoulders.

Front and Back Neck Shaping

PU STS from st holder; cont working in the Basket Weave st until back measures 12½ (14, 16)". BO 14 (16, 18) shoulder sts or place them on a st holder for seam method of preference. Place rem 28 (28, 32) neck sts back on holder until the collar is knitted. Join shoulder seams.

Sleeves

THE SLEEVES are knitted from the top down. They are not knitted in the round, but you can use circular needles if you wish. Measure 5 (5½, 6½)" from shoulder seams in both directions and insert st marker. With RS facing in Color A, PU 48 (52, 60) sts evenly between markers. Leave rem side seam open. Work in basket weave patt until sleeve measures 6 (7, 8)". On next row, beg dec 1 st at each edge EOR 5 (5, 6)x. With rem 38 (42, 48) sts on needle, dec 10 (12, 14) sts evenly across row. Switch to Color B and beg cuff on 28 (30, 34) sts in K1, P1 ribbing for 5 (5, 7) rows. Switch to Color C and work 1 row in K1, P1 ribbing. Work last 2 rows in Color B. BO cuff in K1, P1 ribbing.

Collar

WITH WS facing, in Color B, PU 58 (66, 74) sts from left front, st holder, and right front. Work in K1, P1 ribbing for 12 (13, 14) rows. Work 1 row of K1, P1 ribbing in Color C. Work last 2 rows of K1, P1 ribbing in Color B. BO collar in K1, P1 ribbing.

Finishing

WITH RS facing, place zipper so that the teeth show in front openings. Pin zipper securely in place. Turn garment to WS and hand sew zipper in place, using regular cotton sewing thread. At collar edge, tuck and secure zipper tabs under, facing WS of garment, for a more finished look. Sew sleeve and side seams tog. Add a decorative nautical patch to the left side of the front if desired.

Yarn Jargon

Yarn terms are often expressed in ways that leave even experienced knitters a little bewildered. One such example is the difference between the stitch gauge of a particular yarn as it compares to yarns of other weight. The following is a general rule of thumb.

Fingering Yarn	#1–#4 needles	26–32 sts = 4"
Sport Yarn	#4–#6 needles	23–25 sts = 4"
DK Yarn	#5–#6 needles	21–22 sts = 4"
Worsted Yarn	#5–#8 needles	17–21 sts = 4"
Bulky/Chunky Yarn	#9–17 needles	8–16 sts = 4"

Knitting Terms and Abbreviations

approx	approximately
beg	begin(ning)
BO	bind off
CO	cast on
cn	cable needle
cont	continu(e) (ing) (es)
dec	decreas(e) (ing) (es)
EOR	every other row
est	establish(ed)
inc	increas(e) (ing) (es)
K	knit
P	purl
patt	pattern
psso	pass slip stitch over last stitch worked
PU	pick up
rem	remain(ing)
RS	right side of work
sl	slip stitches from left needle to right needle without working— usually slipped as if to purl, unless otherwise indicated
ssk	slip 1 stitch knitwise, slip 1 stitch knitwise, knit 2 slipped stitches together through back loop—1 stitch has been decreased
st (s)	stitch(es)
St st	stockinette stitch—knit right-side row, purl wrong-side row
tog	together
WS	wrong side of work
wyib	with yarn in back—hold yarn in back while working next stitch
wyif	with yarn in front—hold yarn in front while working next stitch
yo	yarn over needle to make a new stitch—wrap yarn over right needle
x	time(s)
( )	work directions as a group, as many times as indicated
*	starting point for repeating directions, as many times as indicated

Bibliography

Selfridge, Gail. *Sweater Design Workbook*. Loveland, Colo.: Interweave Press, 1991. A helpful informational workbook that includes worksheets of knitter's graph paper in many stitch gauges. An excellent resource for any knitter desiring to use her/his own imagination and originality.

Editors of *Vogue Knitting* magazine. *Vogue Knitting: The Ultimate Knitting Book*. New York: Pantheon Books, 1989.

Walker, Barbara G. *A Treasury of Knitting Patterns*. Pittsville, Wisc.: Schoolhouse Press, 1998. If an aspiring knitter could buy only one knitting book, this should be the one. Barbara Walker is the guru of stitches, and the inspiration that her book provided is woven through the patterns in this book.

About the Authors

Jo Lynne Murchland and Mary H. Bonnette

MARY H. BONNETTE, a native of Minneapolis, began knitting at the age of fourteen for a 4-H project. She quickly moved from following patterns to creating designs of her own. Mary's work has been featured in ski boutiques throughout Colorado and in many knitting publications. Always artistic, Mary continued designing and knitting throughout her college years. She holds a master's degree in hospital administration. Having spent more than twenty years as a health-care administrator, Mary was inspired to design children's wear by the birth of her daughter, Savannah. Although health care has been her career, knitting is her love. She enjoys living in southwest Florida with her husband and daughter, focusing full-time on designing children's knitwear.

Jo Lynne Murchland, originally from West Virginia, began knitting at Denison University in Granville, Ohio. Inspired in childhood by her paternal grandmother, who was an expert seamstress, she learned at an early age to have an appreciation for fabric, fiber, color, and balance. She and her husband settled in Florida over twenty years ago. Prior to 1996, Jo Lynne had worked in both sales and management in the real-estate profession. Knitting has been her passion for many years. With the emergence and success of the Sassy Skein, she has been given the opportunity to focus on a career in a field she loves. Color, texture, and originality has set Jo Lynne's garments apart from the ordinary. Just ask her granddaughters, Ashleigh and Rachel, who now enjoy wearing and modeling her creations.

NEW AND BESTSELLING TITLES FROM

America's Best-Loved Craft & Hobby Books™

America's Best-Loved Quilt Books®

QUILTING
from That Patchwork Place®, an imprint of Martingale & Company™

Appliqué
Artful Appliqué
Colonial Appliqué
Red and Green: An Appliqué Tradition
Rose Sampler Supreme
Your Family Heritage: Projects in
  Appliqué

Baby Quilts
Appliqué for Baby
The Quilted Nursery
Quilts for Baby: Easy as ABC
More Quilts for Baby: Easy as ABC
Even More Quilts for Baby: Easy as ABC

Holiday Quilts
Easy and Fun Christmas Quilts
Favorite Christmas Quilts from That
  Patchwork Place
Paper Piece a Merry Christmas
A Snowman's Family Album Quilt
Welcome to the North Pole

Learning to Quilt
Basic Quiltmaking Techniques for:
  Borders and Bindings
  Curved Piecing
  Divided Circles
  Eight-Pointed Stars
  Hand Appliqué
  Machine Appliqué
  Strip Piecing
The Joy of Quilting
The Quilter's Handbook
Your First Quilt Book (or it should be!)

Paper Piecing
50 Fabulous Paper-Pieced Stars
A Quilter's Ark
Easy Machine Paper Piecing
Needles and Notions
Paper-Pieced Curves
Show Me How to Paper Piece

Rotary Cutting
101 Fabulous Rotary-Cut Quilts
365 Quilt Blocks a Year Perpetual
  Calendar
Fat Quarter Quilts
Lap Quilting Lives!
Quick Watercolor Quilts
Quilts from Aunt Amy
Spectacular Scraps
Time-Crunch Quilts

Small & Miniature Quilts
Bunnies By The Bay Meets Little Quilts
Celebrate! with Little Quilts
Easy Paper-Pieced Miniatures
Little Quilts All Through the House

CRAFTS
From Martingale & Company

300 Papermaking Recipes
The Art of Handmade Paper and
  Collage
The Art of Stenciling
Creepy Crafty Halloween
Gorgeous Paper Gifts
Grow Your Own Paper
Stamp with Style
Wedding Ribbonry

KNITTING
From Martingale & Company

Comforts of Home
Fair Isle Sweaters Simplified
Knit It Your Way
Simply Beautiful Sweaters
Two Sticks and a String
The Ultimate Knitter's Guide
Welcome Home: Kaffe Fassett

COLLECTOR'S COMPASS™
From Martingale & Company

20th Century Glass
'50s Decor
Barbie® Doll
Jewelry

Coming to *Collector's Compass* Spring 2001:

20th Century Dinnerware
American Coins
Movie Star Collectibles
'60s Decor

Our books are available at bookstores and your favorite craft, fabric, yarn, and antiques retailers. If you don't see the title you're looking for, visit us at **www.martingale-pub.com** or contact us at:

1-800-426-3126
International: 1-425-483-3313
Fax: 1-425-486-7596
E-mail: info@martingale-pub.com

For more information and a full list of our titles, visit our Web site or call for a free catalog.